telling America's Story

A History of The Henry Ford

THE
DONNING COMPANY
PUBLISHERS

telling America's Story

A History of The Henry Ford

By Jeanine Head Miller, Judith E. Endelman, Donna R. Braden, and Nancy Villa Bryk · Judith E. Endelman and Wendy Metros, editors

The Donning Company Publishers
184 Business Park Drive, Suite 206
Virginia Beach, VA 23462

Steve Mull, General Manager
Barbara Buchanan, Office Manager
Pamela Koch, Senior Editor
Scott Rule, Graphic Designer
Derek Eley, Imaging Artist

Debbie Dowell, Project Research Coordinator
Tonya Hannink, Marketing Specialist
Pamela Engelhard, Marketing Advisor

G. Bradley Martin, Project Director

20900 Oakwood Boulevard
Dearborn, Michigan 48124-5029
313.982.6001
TheHenryFord.org

Library of Congress Cataloging-in-Publication Data

Telling America's story : a history of the Henry Ford / by Jeanine Head Miller ... [et al.] ; Judith E. Endelman and Wendy Metros, editors.
p. cm.
Includes bibliographical references and index.
ISBN 978-1-57864-577-0 (hard cover : alk. paper)
1. Henry Ford (Organization)--History. 2. Automobiles--United States--History. I. Miller, Jeanine Head, 1955- II. Endelman, Judith E. III. Metros, Wendy.
T180.D4H465 2009
607'.3477433--dc22
2009021291

Printed in the United States of America at Walsworth Publishing Company

table of Contents

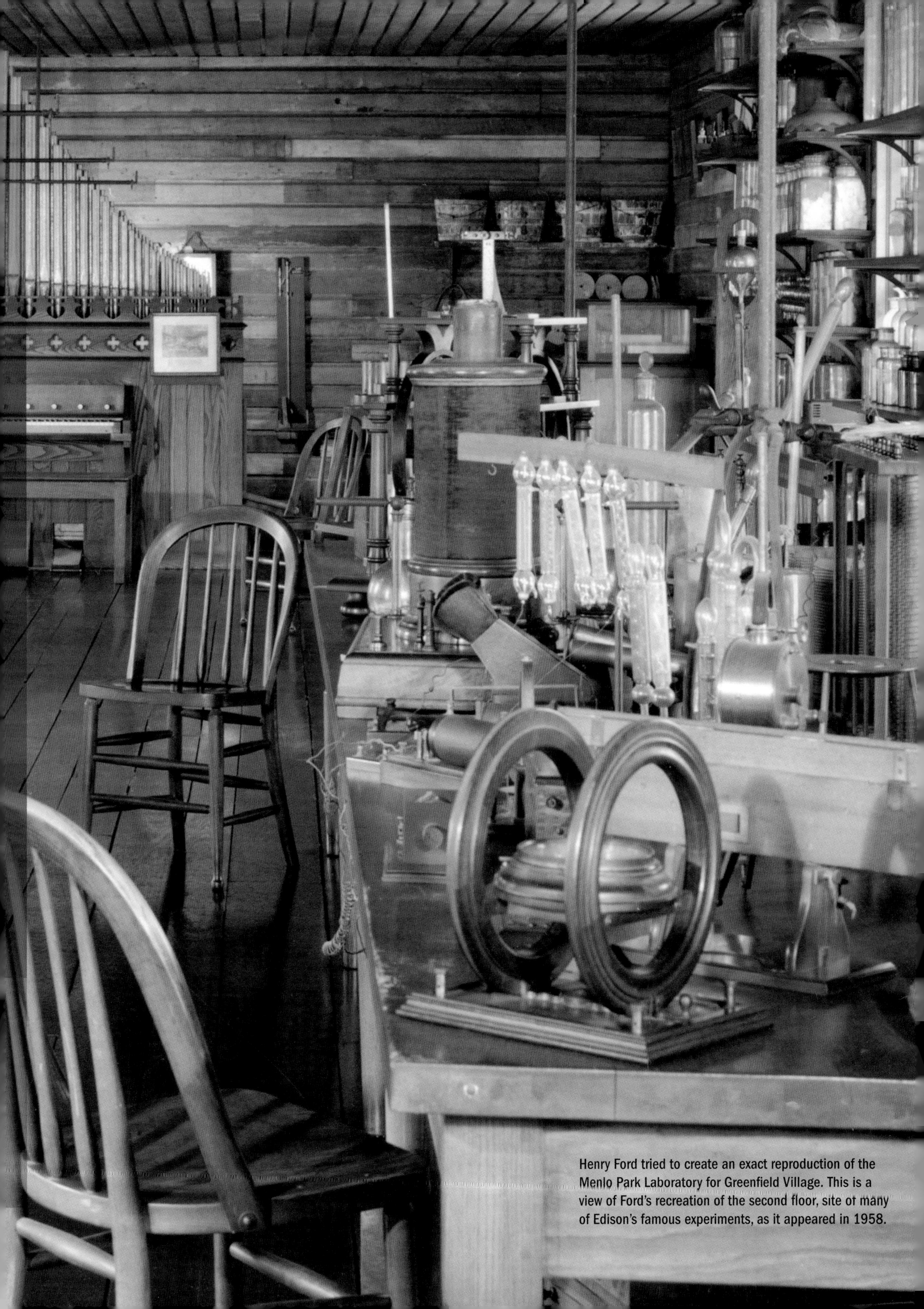

Henry Ford tried to create an exact reproduction of the Menlo Park Laboratory for Greenfield Village. This is a view of Ford's recreation of the second floor, site of many of Edison's famous experiments, as it appeared in 1958.

foreword

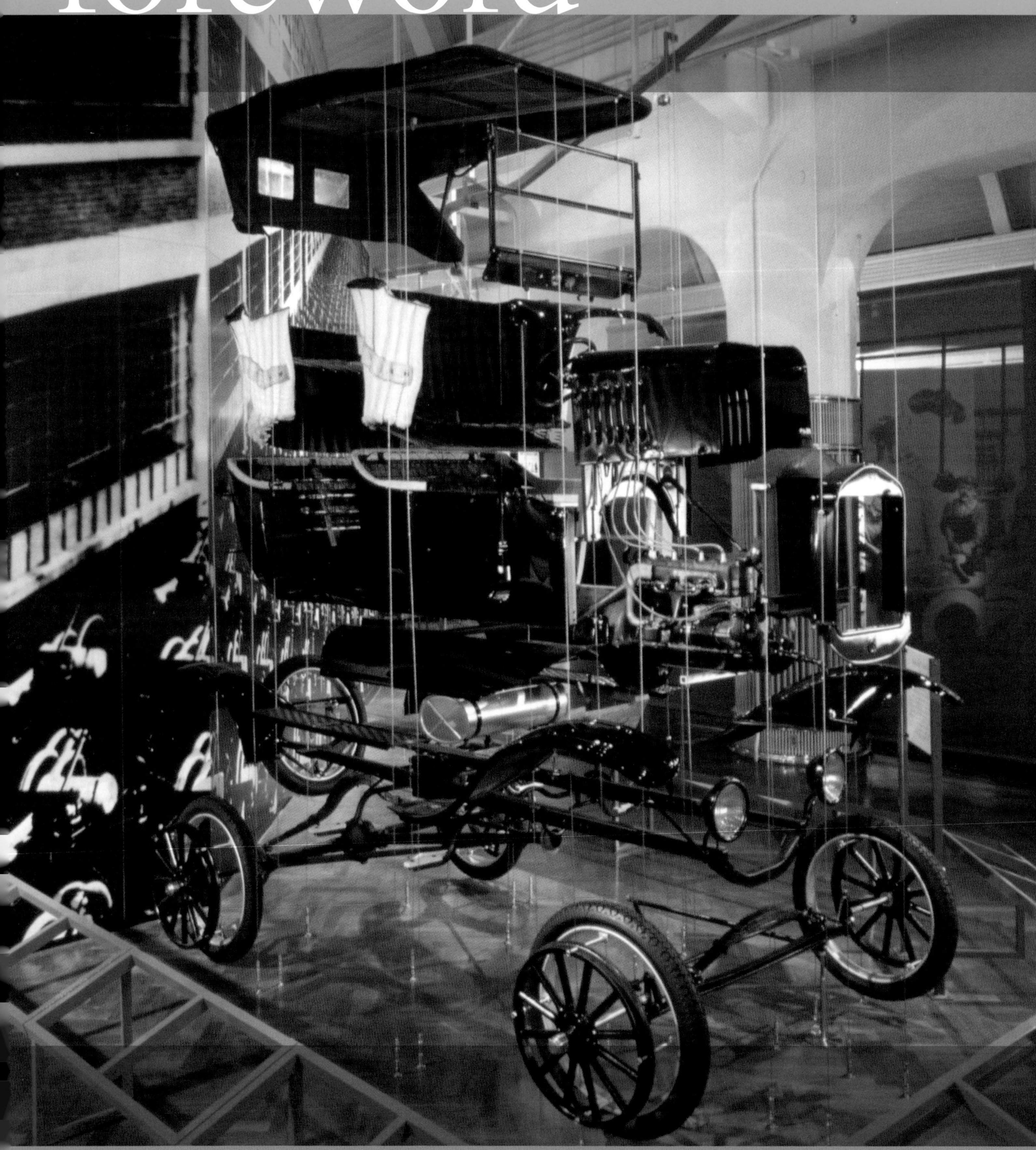

An "exploded Model T" in the *Made in America* exhibit in Henry Ford Museum reveals all the parts that went into the assembly of the car.

Henry Ford once famously said, "*the only history that is worth a tinker's damn is the history we make today.*"

Coupled with his faith in what he called the "common genius of the American people," these two core beliefs remain the driving principles of an extraordinary institution known today as The Henry Ford.

For Ford, the American genius was rooted in its entrepreneurial spirit and best represented in those American innovations and inventions that eliminated drudgery, improved quality of life, and allowed working people the means to participate in and prosper from a growing economy. He believed that these were the elements of the true history of America with which our youth should become familiar, and that they could learn that history best, not simply by reading texts, but by doing. And so, he created an institution—this institution—to be a hands-on learning environment about America's history . . . and its future.

In 1929, Henry Ford, in honor of his friend and mentor, Thomas Edison, who, in Ford's mind, epitomized the American spirit of innovation, formally dedicated The Edison Institute, now known as The Henry Ford. Since its founding, the institution has become widely recognized as a unique and inspiring visitor destination, a cherished National Historic Landmark, and an innovative educational resource housing what the American Association of Museums deemed "*the finest collection ever assembled documenting the American experience.*"

In keeping with its founding vision, The Henry Ford will be a force for fueling the spirit of American innovation and inspiring a "can-do" culture. It will accomplish this through its collections initiatives, exhibit and program development, public programs, and by developing successful and replicable models of educational reform. It presents and connects the stories of America's past and present doers, makers, tinkerers, and risk-takers, with America's historical, contemporary, and future challenges and opportunities.

It's what we do today, informed and inspired by the past, that can help us shape a better future. And that was, and remains, the essential value proposition of The Henry Ford. I hope that you will enjoy this brief history of our organization and I invite you to become a part of our ongoing efforts to help chart America's future through the illumination of its past.

Patricia

Patricia E. Mooradian
President, The Henry Ford

acknowledgments

Chemical bottles line the shelves of the Menlo Park Laboratory, just as they did in Edison's day.

Beyond the four authors whose names appear on the title page are many people who contributed to the production of this history of The Henry Ford, written to commemorate our eightieth anniversary.

Our thanks go to our internal review team—Terri Anderson, Patricia Mooradian, Carol Kendra, Christian Overland, Cheryl Preston, George Moroz, and Steve Hamp—who provided wise editorial guidance and direction.

Jim Orr and Margaret Hoover were relentless in locating the dozens of photographs that enliven this book. We also want to thank photographers Rudy Ruzicska, Michelle Andonian, Gary Malerba, and the late Philippe Halsman for creating many of these wonderful images. We are grateful to Jim Johnson who helped to consolidate much of the information on the programs and activities of the past twenty years. Wes Hardin guided the early phases of this project, and we thank him for his devotion to it.

It was Ralph Waldo Emerson who remarked that "an institution is the lengthened shadow of one man." Though many have contributed to the greatness of The Henry Ford, the collection that Henry Ford created and his vision continue to nourish the staff and visitors to this great institution.

All photographs are from the collections of The Henry Ford.

Judith E. Endelman and Wendy Metros
Editors

CHAPTER 1

A contemporary view of the second floor of the restored Menlo Park Laboratory in Greenfield Village.

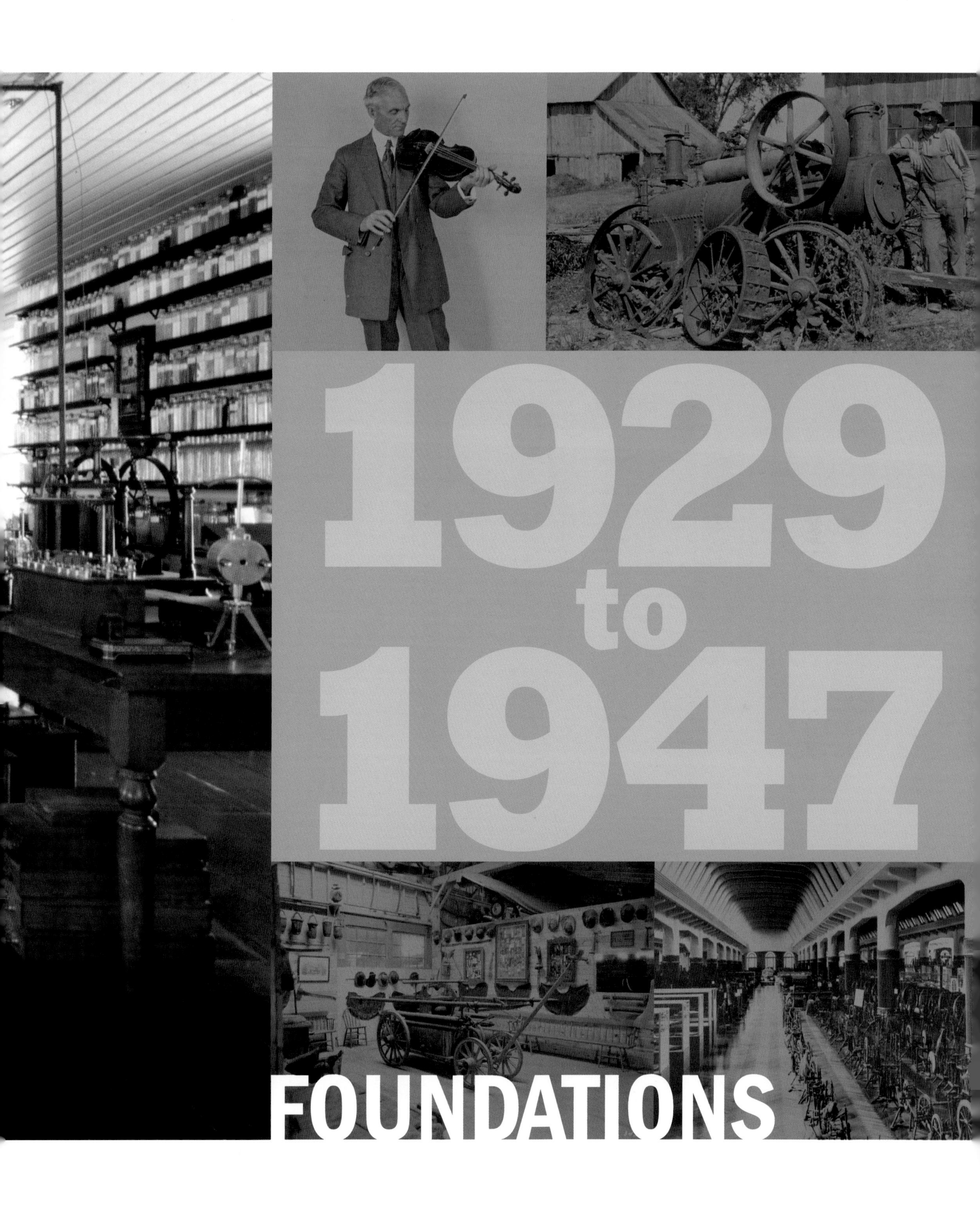
1929
to
1947
FOUNDATIONS

“history Is More or Less Bunk”

“By looking at the things that people used and the way they lived, a better and truer impression can be gained in an hour than could be had from a month of reading.”

– Henry Ford, *New York Times Magazine*, April 5, 1931

Henry Ford was one of the most successful industrialists of the twentieth century.

His Model T, "the car for the great multitude," was introduced in 1908 and was an immediate success. In 1913, he debuted the moving assembly line at his factory in Highland Park, Michigan, and by early 1914, he doubled the standard wage of his automobile workers to the unheard-of amount of five dollars a day. By 1920, the Model T constituted nearly half of all cars on America's roads.

The world was on wheels, and it was changing. The wide adoption of the Model T in the early twentieth century helped to accelerate the rapid social change that had begun in the late nineteenth century. The automobile brought industrialization and waves of southern and eastern European immigrants to America.

With the growth of cities came the decline of rural areas, and many Americans began to covet a simpler time, when all seemed to share the same traditional values.

In 1921, Henry Ford posed by a Model T, the car that changed America and made his fortune.

This longing for an American past found expression in a growing interest in American decorative arts, paintings, and other art objects. Members of the American elite, who had previously spent their fortunes on European and English paintings, sculptures, and decorative arts, began to develop an interest in Americana. Henry Francis du Pont, for example, collected English and European antique furnishings until a 1923 visit to the Shelburne, Vermont, home of Joseph and Electra Havemeyer Webb, the noted folk art collectors, convinced him to collect only Americana.

Fine American furniture, porcelain, glassware, paintings, rare books, and maps—these were the kinds of objects that attracted most collectors.

Except for collectors like Henry Ford. Ford was more interested in tools and machinery than he was in accumulating pieces of art.

As early as 1912, he was collecting "relics" such as wagons and threshing machines that represented American industrial progress, as well as objects that reflected a world that was vanishing with every Model T that rolled off the assembly line.

(Opposite) With horticulturist Luther Burbank's shovel firmly in the wet cement, Thomas Edison added his flamboyant signature to the museum cornerstone, September 27, 1928, representing the union of agriculture and industry.

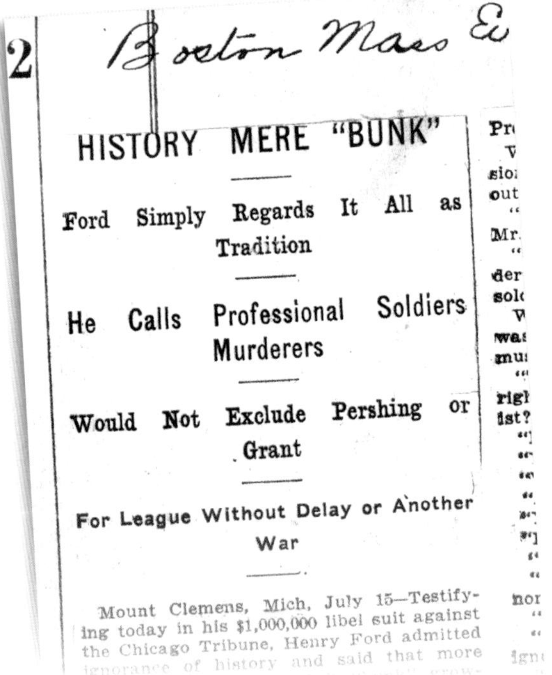

HISTORY MERE "BUNK"

Ford Simply Regards It All as Tradition

He Calls Professional Soldiers Murderers

Would Not Exclude Pershing or Grant

For League Without Delay or Another War

Mount Clemens, Mich, July 15—Testifying today in his $1,000,000 libel suit against the Chicago Tribune, Henry Ford admitted

Ford repeated the phrase he had first uttered in 1916, "history is more or less bunk," at the 1919 libel trial against the *Chicago Tribune*.

Unlike most wealthy collectors, Ford's interests were not aesthetic but evolutionary. He saw in humble machines an expression of the "genius of the American people" and a reflection of American progress. To Ford, who was not much of a reader, objects were a way to learn about the past without reading about it. Ford enthusiastically collected machinery and other inventions that had changed the everyday life of ordinary Americans. He collected steam engines, tractors, stoves, and other industrial objects to enable Americans to appreciate "the actual development of American industry from the earliest days." In addition to collecting historic machinery, he also acquired examples of contemporary inventions that were changing people's lives, such as radios, engines, and household appliances. He sought out items that reminded him of his own childhood, such as McGuffey Readers, and objects that reflected a way of life that was quickly slipping away. He collected items that belonged to his personal heroes, such as Thomas Edison and Abraham Lincoln. He believed that one could feel the presence of great people through their possessions.

Although no one knows for sure when Ford first decided to turn his private passion into a public institution, his 1919 libel suit against the *Chicago Tribune* seems to have provided a catalyst. The newspaper had called Ford an "anarchist" and "ignorant idealist" after the paper mistakenly accused Ford Motor Company of failing to support workers who were called up for National Guard duty to fight Mexican revolutionary Pancho Villa.

In a pensive moment between trial sessions, Ford relaxed in a wheat field near the courthouse.

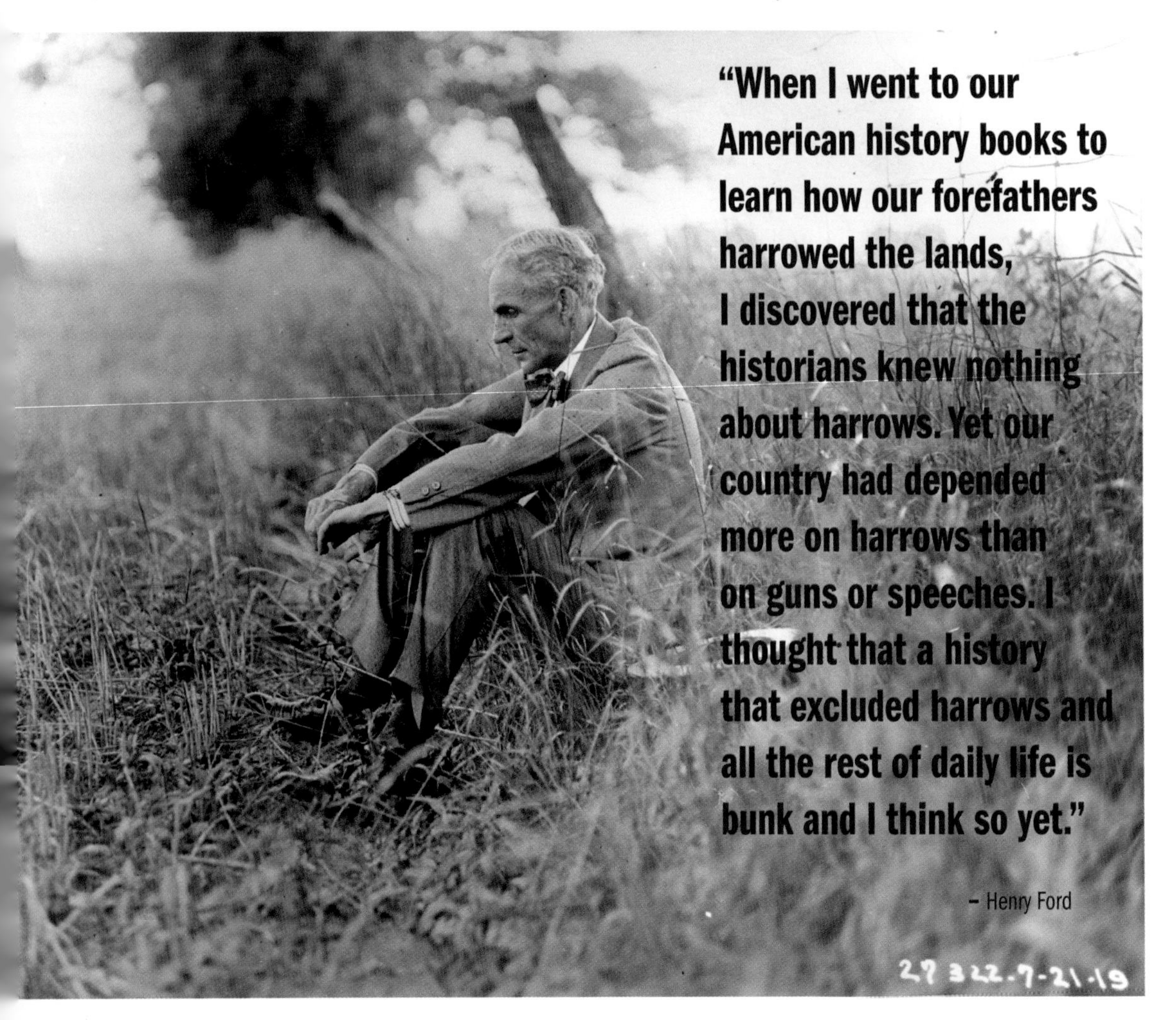

As the trial progressed, *Tribune* lawyers mercilessly examined Ford on a variety of schoolbook topics, history in particular. Ford answered question after question incorrectly. After expressing contempt for the emphasis on memorized facts, Ford finally replied in exasperation: "History is more or less bunk. It's tradition. We don't want tradition. We want to live in the present, and the only history that is worth a tinker's damn is the history we make today." The simplistic epigram "History is bunk" stuck in the public mind.

The truth is, Henry Ford never really believed that "history is bunk." What he did believe was that the kind of history taught in schools, the history that emphasized kings and generals—and omitted ordinary folks and the tools of everyday life—was useless.

Ford believed that the everyday objects he loved to collect told the truth not recorded in written histories, and he declared that these collections reflected the true history of America. On the way home from the trial, Ford said to his secretary, Ernest Liebold: "I'm going to start up a museum and give people a true picture of the development of the country. That's the only history that is worth observing. We'll show the people what actually existed in years gone by, and we'll show the actual development of American industry from the earliest days."

FACT:

After nearly fourteen weeks of testimony, the jury found in favor of Henry Ford and ordered the *Chicago Tribune* to pay costs. The jury awarded Ford damages of just six cents. Ford's ignorance and lack of book learning had struck a sympathetic chord with the American public.

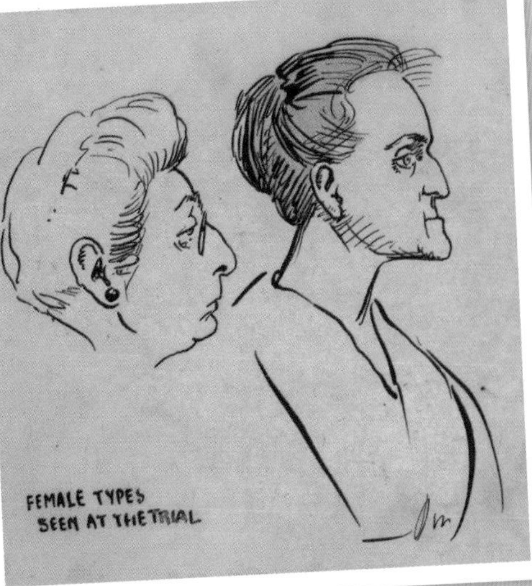

During the *Chicago Tribune* trial, Irving Bacon (Henry Ford's personal artist) sat in the courtroom sketching the participants. Bacon captured the judge, lawyers, members of the jury, and spectators. Only Henry Ford is missing.

restoring the Past

"I never had any particular love for the farm. It was the mother on the farm I loved."

– Henry Ford, "Ford Renews Old Home as Holy Shrine" in *Literary Digest*, 1923

Henry Ford was drawn into thinking about the past—his own past—when he was in his fifties.

In 1919, he contemplated the importance of his own birthplace when a road improvement project required that the farmhouse be either moved two hundred yards from its original location or destroyed.

Ford decided to move the house and restore it to the way it looked at the time of his mother's death in 1876, when he was thirteen. Ford personally took charge of the birthplace restoration, meticulously recreating the details of the house. He worked tirelessly to find original or similar furnishings. For example, Ford recalled sitting by a Starlight stove in the dining room as a child. After an eighteen-month-long nationwide search involving stove companies and Ford automobile dealers, Ford discovered the exact make and model rusting on a Stockbridge, Michigan, porch. Dismantling the $25 acquisition, Ford loaded the stove into his car for the journey back to Dearborn. To find dishes to match the red transfer ware his mother had used, he had the site excavated to find any remaining pieces of broken pottery. When Ford couldn't find the precise pattern for purchase, he had dishes replicated from the pottery shards.

He dedicated the restoration to Mary Litogot Ford's memory and her teachings, particularly noting her love of family, her belief in the value of hard work, in learning "not from school books but from life," and her belief in trusting one's intuition. His mother had encouraged his early tinkering and youthful inventions, and he felt sure she had set him on his unique path.

When the restoration of his childhood home was completed, people were awestruck by its authenticity. It seemed remarkable to him, and others, how a recreated environment could catapult one into another time and place.

Henry Ford on the porch of his restored childhood home in 1923.

In 1923, he bought and preserved the red brick Scotch Settlement School that he had attended as a child. Henry Ford kept the building on its original site while he supervised every detail of its restoration.

Henry Ford's restoration of his birthplace received extensive press coverage. Not surprisingly, Americans deluged the wealthy man with

(Opposite) Henry Ford's birthplace after its restoration in 1923. The Dearborn, Michigan, farmhouse was built by his father, William Ford, about 1860. Henry Ford was born in a second-floor bedroom on July 30, 1863.

(Above)
Henry Ford's mother, Mary Litogot Ford, as a young woman.

(Right) Henry Ford at age two.

(Below) Ford had his mother's dishes reproduced from pottery shards found at the property.

pleas of assistance for preservation projects of their own. Although Ford turned down most requests for assistance, a few caught his fancy.

He turned down Reverend William Goodwin from Williamsburg, Virginia, who wrote requesting five million dollars to fund the restoration of Williamsburg, the Colonial-era Virginia capital. Ford was more interested in creating his own village, which would include buildings from different time periods and places. Reverend Goodwin found his benefactor in John D. Rockefeller.

Ford did agree, however, to assist in the restoration of the 1686 Wayside Inn of Sudbury, Massachusetts, west of Boston. Henry Wadsworth Longfellow had made the inn famous in his *Tales of a Wayside Inn*. The author's "Psalm of Life," read by Ford in the McGuffey Readers of his youth, was among the industrialist's favorite inspirational verses. Ford purchased the inn for $65,000, restoring and refurnishing it at significant expense. He bought up much surrounding land and even diverted the Boston Post Road to keep automobile traffic from ruining the bucolic setting.

He hired prominent antiques dealer Israel Sack to fill the inn with colonial furnishings, including some relating to such American patriots as John Hancock and George Washington. Henry Ford thought that history came alive when one could gaze upon the furniture of great men and hear about their lives.

Ford clearly contemplated even grander plans for the Wayside Inn and its surrounding property. A "Proposed Development of a Colonial Village of South Sudbury, Massachusetts . . . done at the Lowthorpe School of Landscape Architecture," in 1926 shows a "village" composed of the Wayside Inn, houses, a church, a mill, and other buildings, as well as commemorative vignettes of the "midnight ride of Paul Revere," "the babbling brook of Longfellow," George Washington taking command of the continental troops, and

The Wayside Inn in the mid-1920s, after its restoration.

(Right) Henry and Clara Ford periodically visited the Wayside Inn, whose doors had been opened to the public. By 1927, however, Henry's attention increasingly turned to his plans for his historical village and museum in Dearborn.

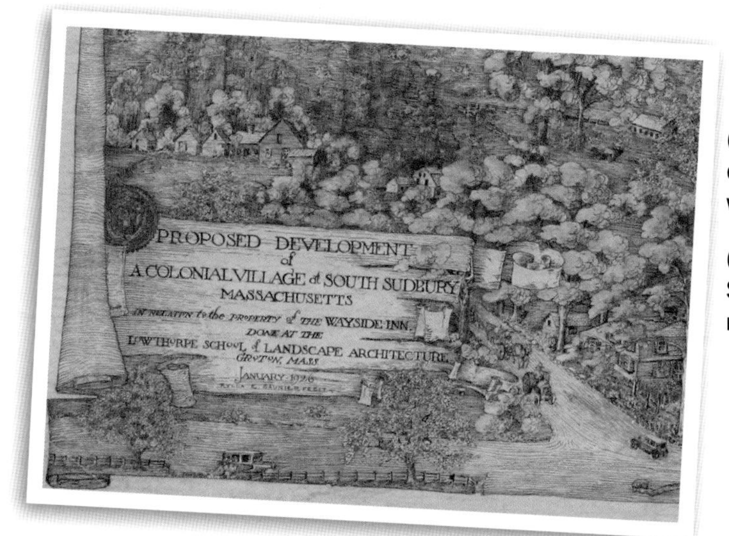

(Left) In 1926, the press reported that Ford was to "build an old time town" on the Wayside Inn property. This detail from an artist's rendering showed what Ford's proposed colonial village might have looked like.

(Below) Not far from Dearborn was the 1836 Botsford Inn, known then as the Sixteen Mile House. This is how the inn appeared in 1900, before Henry Ford restored it in the mid-1920s.

(Left) Henry Ford began his schooling at the Scotch Settlement School in 1871. After Ford purchased and restored the building, he used it as a preschool to promote a progressive mix of old and new teaching methods. He moved it to Greenfield Village in 1929.

others. Although the plan was never realized, Ford may have been working out ideas that were later revealed in Greenfield Village.

Closer to home, Ford refurbished the old Botsford Inn, on Grand River Avenue, in Farmington, Michigan, in 1924. The inn had once served nineteenth-century travelers en route from Detroit to Lansing. Ford's staff sought out old-timers who remembered the inn in its heyday and used their recollections to help furnish the place. Ford added a maple floor to the ballroom and, for a while, held old-fashioned dances there.

FACT:
Although Skansen, the first "open air museum," opened in Sweden in 1891, Greenfield Village is considered America's first open air museum.

"In explaining Mr. Ford's interest in the past, I think that in every person, after they reach a certain age, they begin to reminisce . . . in Mr. Ford's case, he was able to carry it further than the average person."

- Ernest Liebold, Secretary to Henry Ford, *Reminiscences*

collector at Heart

"We want to have something of everything . . . one of these days the collection will have its own museum at Dearborn, and there we shall reproduce the life of the country in its every age."

– Henry Ford, *Garden and Home Builder*, July 1926

By 1924, Ford's avid collecting of "everyday Americana" began to border on an obsession.

With his collecting efforts focused on items and subjects he loved, Ford found himself combing the country for significant timepieces, McGuffey Readers, farm equipment, and fine classical Stradivari and Guarneri violins.

He began to amass huge amounts of items that were already considered quaint in the early 1920s, so much so that his growing collection outgrew its designated space in Ford's office and had to be moved into Ford Motor Company's Building 13, a vacated tractor assembly area. The objects represented almost every aspect of everyday life—agricultural machinery, steam engines, furniture, guns, clothing, and automobiles. Pieces from Ford's collecting habit were packed, stacked, and hung from the rafters. Even Ford's restoration projects—his childhood home, the Botsford Inn, and the Wayside Inn—were used for storage.

The Fords enjoyed sharing their growing pile of relics with others by displaying some of their favorite pieces in their home. Mr. and Mrs. Ford were also known to lend their historical objects for local events and displays. Household and agricultural antiques from Ford's collection graced a downtown Detroit store in September 1928.

After the public learned that Henry Ford was collecting objects for a museum, antique dealers as well as ordinary people began to flood Ford's office with letters offering to give or sell him antiques of all shapes and sizes. At Building 13, Frank Campsall and Ford's other secretaries read virtually every offer that came across their desks. They then discussed the proposed acquisitions with Ford.

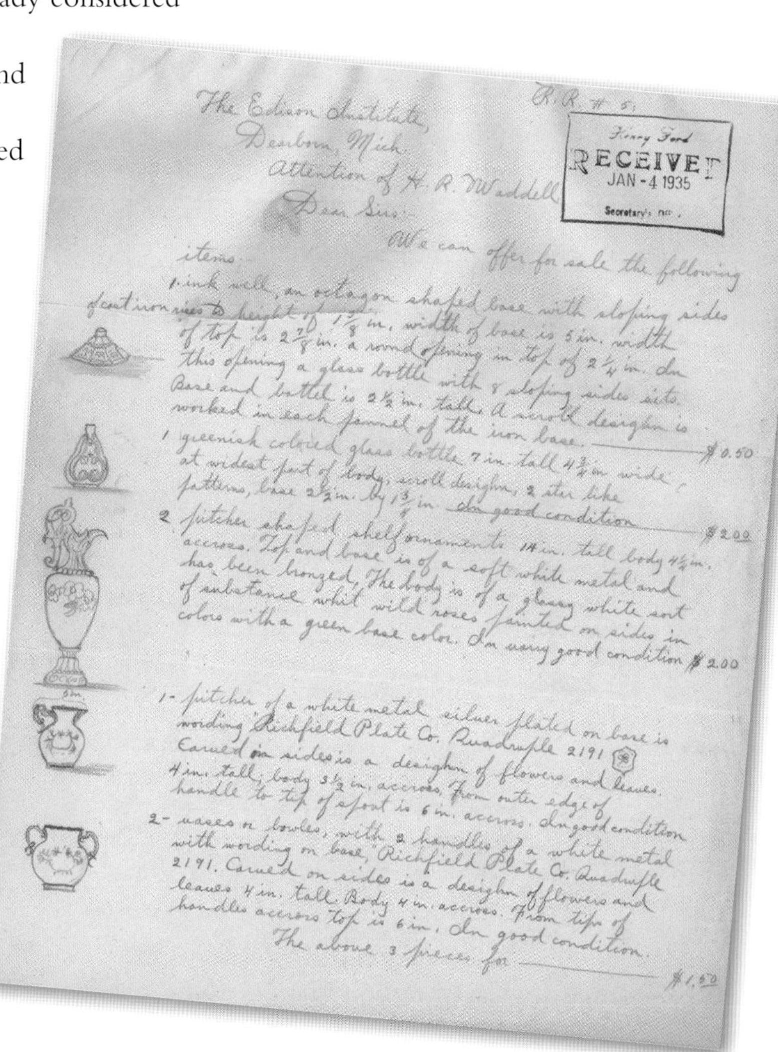

R. R. # 5;

Henry Ford
RECEIVED
JAN - 4 1935
Secretary's no.

The Edison Institute,
Dearborn, Mich.
Attention of H. R. Waddell,
Dear Sirs:-
We can offer for sale the following items.

1 ink well, an octagon shaped base with sloping sides of cast iron rises to height of 1 5/8 in. width of base is 5 in. width of top is 2 7/8 in. a round opening in top of 2 1/4 in. In this opening a glass bottle with 8 sloping sides sits. Base and bottel is 2 1/2 in. tall. A scroll deisghn is worked in each pannel of the iron base. ——— $0.50

1 greenish colored glass bottle 7 in. tall 4 3/4 in wide at widest part of body, scroll deisghn, 2 star like patterns, base 2 1/2 in. by 1 3/4 in. In good condition ——— $2.00

2 pitcher shaped shelf ornaments 14 in. tall body 4 1/4 in. accross. Top and base is of a soft white metal and has been bronzed, The body is of a glassy white sort of substance whit wild roses painted on sides in colors with a green base color. In vairy good condition $2.00

1- pitcher of a white metal silver plated on base is wording "Richfield Plate Co. Quadruple 2191 Carved on sides is a deisghn of flowers and leaves. 4 in. tall; body 3 1/2 in. accross, from outer edge of handle to tip of spout is 6 in. accross. In good condition

2- vases or bowles, with 2 handles of a white metal with wording on base, "Richfield Plate Co. Quadruple 2191. Carved on sides is a deisghn of flowers and leaves 4 in. tall. Body 4 in. accross. From tips of handles accross top is 6 in. In good condition.

The above 3 pieces for ——— $1.50

Instead of sending photographs of items for sale, this Muncie, Indiana, antique dealer drew them.

(Opposite) Three of the men responsible for responding to proposed offers stood amid their latest acquisitions in 1928. At left is Frank Campsall, a secretary who responded to written inquiries of donations and purchases. In the center is Charles Newton, a lawyer who handled the legal transactions in Ford's historical projects and often accompanied Ford on his countryside searches for old farm equipment. Henry Ford stands at the right.

Henry Ford did not rely solely on his collecting expeditions or offers from the interested public. He hired agents to help him find and acquire the kinds of objects he felt were important to preserve. These men ferreted out relics and negotiated for old buildings. They kept journals and corresponded regularly to relay their finds. William W. Taylor, whom Ford met while restoring the Wayside Inn, combed his native New England for furniture, tools, carriages, and buildings for Ford's collection. Taylor kept a detailed journal and sent in weekly reports. The Wayside Inn project also introduced Ford to Israel Sack, a well-known Boston antique dealer, who eventually acquired many extraordinary pieces of early American furniture for Ford. Jim Bishop, an expert in early electrical equipment and an old friend of Ford, amassed the museum's unparalleled electrical collections. Bishop reported that Henry Ford asked him to acquire "at least one of every device . . . ever made to generate, conduct, control and use electricity. . . and bring them to Dearborn."

Henry Ford also collected more recent items, particularly if they reflected American innovation.

This July 1941 newspaper cartoon noted Henry Ford's inclination to collect objects of everyday life in enormous numbers.

(Above) Jim Bishop, an expert in early electrical equipment and an old friend of Henry Ford, amassed the museum's unparalleled electrical collections.

In October 1943, Sikorsky landed his prototype helicopter in front of a crowd of visitors and dignitaries and donated it to the museum.

"We would make visits around New England . . . and, without previous plan in mind, visit people and see what they had . . . We bought Lawton's house . . . lock-stock-and-barrel, and it was just loaded with antiques."

- Harold Cordell, Assistant Secretary to Henry Ford, *Reminiscences*

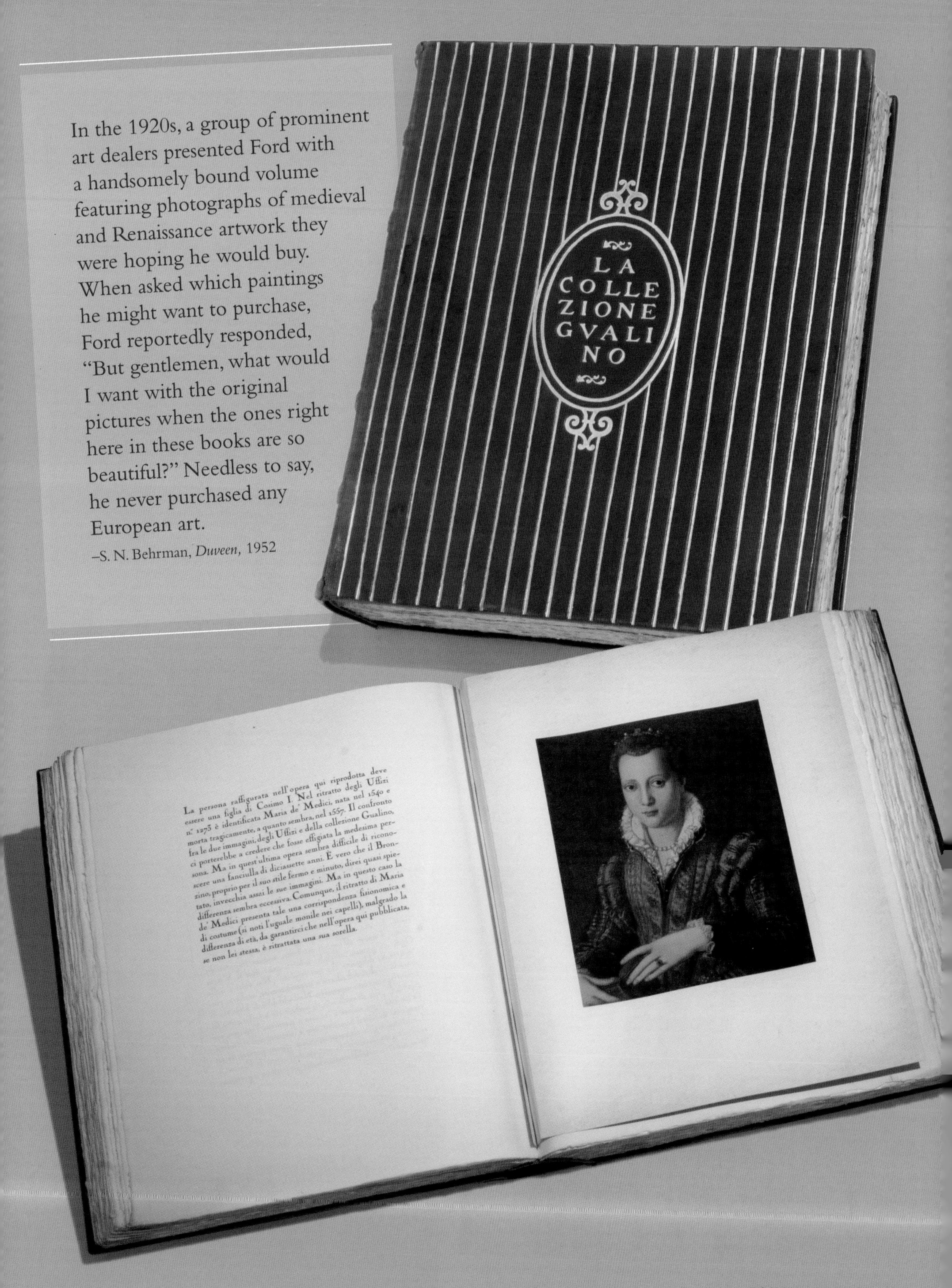

In the 1920s, a group of prominent art dealers presented Ford with a handsomely bound volume featuring photographs of medieval and Renaissance artwork they were hoping he would buy. When asked which paintings he might want to purchase, Ford reportedly responded, "But gentlemen, what would I want with the original pictures when the ones right here in these books are so beautiful?" Needless to say, he never purchased any European art.

–S. N. Behrman, *Duveen*, 1952

(Right) This colorful cupboard was made in Hadley, Massachusetts, in the 1710s for Hannah Barnard. Henry Ford purchased it in 1936.

(Below) One of Henry Ford's McGuffey Readers.

(Left) This 1923 photo is marked "Clocks for Mr. Ford's Office."

(Below) This Ames engine was purchased from this Michigan farmer and later restored for exhibition.

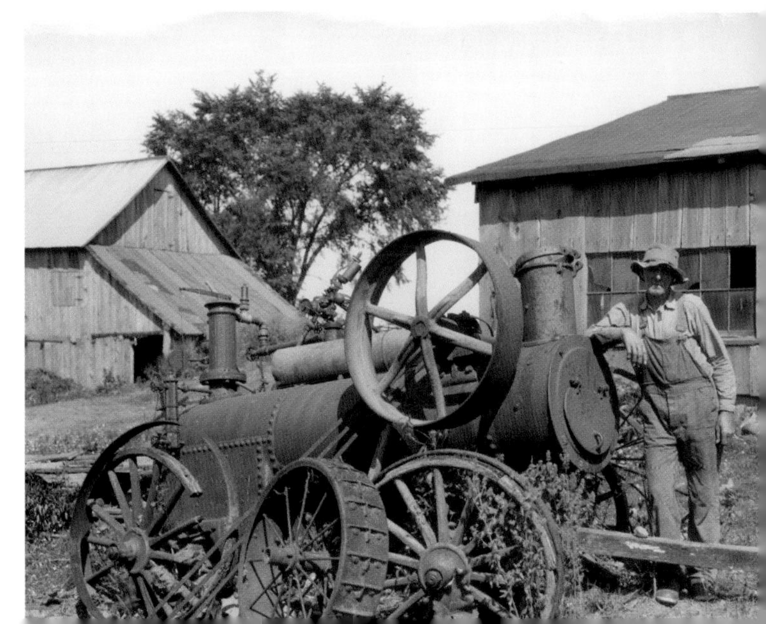

Trainloads of goods intended for the museum arrived in Dearborn almost daily—sometimes by the train car full. Henry Ford had become the largest collector of Americana in the world.

Not all of the objects he gathered were American. Henry Ford also sought British objects that he felt represented America's industrial and cultural roots. In 1928, Ford hired Herbert Morton, plant engineer at the Ford Motor Company in England, to find and acquire significant early British steam engines, watches, furniture, and even buildings.

Henry Ford wanted to tell the story of industrial progress by beginning with the earliest successes of the Industrial Revolution. With Morton's assistance, Ford acquired the oldest known surviving steam engine, a Newcomen atmospheric engine that had been installed in the Cannel Mine in Lancashire, England, about 1765. Ford wanted to acquire Robert Stephenson's Rocket, which had been built in 1829 for the Liverpool and Manchester Railway in England, and was the most famous of Britain's early surviving locomotives. However, the Rocket was part of the London Science Museum's collection. In 1929, Ford commissioned a working replica from the original builders, Robert Stephenson and Company.

Henry and Clara's travels in England had acquainted them with the charming stone architecture of the Cotswold region. In 1929, Herbert Morton found an early seventeenth century Cotswold cottage and barn located near Chedworth in Gloucestershire that Ford purchased for Greenfield Village. The cottage and its adjacent barn, along with a seventeenth century blacksmith shop, were disassembled stone by

Although Henry Ford loved to play the fiddle, he was not a skilled player. He treated his valuable violins with surprising casualness, keeping them in a closet in his Fair Lane home.

After Abraham Lincoln's assassination in April 1865, the United States government confiscated the rocking chair he was seated in at Ford's Theatre the night he was shot. In 1929, the Lincoln chair was returned to Blanche Chapman Ford, widow of Ford's Theater manager Harry Clay Ford to whom the chair had belonged. Initially, Blanche Ford offered the chair for sale to Henry Ford for his museum. The offer was turned down by one of Ford's secretaries with the explanation that Mr. Ford did not desire such a gruesome object for his new museum. Henry Ford probably never saw the letter. Blanche Ford then decided to put the chair up for auction. Knowing of Ford's interest in furniture associated with great Americans, Israel Sack bid on the chair, purchased it for $2,400, and sold it to Henry Ford.

Here, the Lincoln chair is shown being unpacked from its shipping crate. For many years, the rocker was displayed in the Logan County Courthouse in Greenfield Village, along with other Lincoln-related furniture and documents.

"Driving in a car, Mr. Ford would stop many times to look at antique equipment or machinery setting in a field. He'd see an engine or something and say, 'Let's go over and see what it is. Let's take a look at it.'"

- Ernest Liebold, Secretary to Henry Ford, *Reminiscences*

stone, put in sixty-seven English train cars, and shipped to Greenfield Village. Morton arranged for a team of English builders to come with the 475,000 pounds of limestone and assist with the reassembly of the Cotswold buildings in Greenfield Village. However, Henry Ford and the Englishmen did not agree on how the buildings were to be reconstructed and he sent the Englishmen home. Ford's own crews completed the work.

The clock figures on Sir John Bennett's Jewelry Store were a much-loved landmark on busy Cheapside Street in London from 1846 to 1929. Always a lover of clocks, this famous clock caught Henry Ford's eye, and in 1929, plans to rebuild the storefront offered Ford a chance to buy not only the clock figures and mechanism but the entire building façade. Morton facilitated this purchase as well.

In letters written to Frank Campsall and Ernest Liebold, two of Henry Ford's secretaries, in 1933, Herbert Morton wrote that his "strange

(Far left) Henry Ford had his office in Ford Motor Company's Engineering Building. He stored his growing collections in the adjacent tractor assembly plant known as Building 13. Clara Ford would sometimes pull a few of her favorite antiques out of storage and arrange them in attractive displays in the Engineering Building.

(Left above) Building 13 served as a halfway house for Ford's collection until a year or two after The Edison Institute Museum's dedication in 1929. Ford's staff used Building 13 to lay out museum artifact displays and village building interiors.

(Left below) A costumed Henry and Clara Ford enjoy an elegant ride from days past during Dearborn's Fourth of July parade in 1924. The pageant featured eighteen horse-drawn vehicles from Ford's collection.

commission" allowed him to relive "the days when Steam was giving a new birth to the world . . . lifted a treasure from the Cotswold Hills and took a slice from the heart of London itself." For Morton, it was a grand adventure—and the perfect job.

By the mid-1920s, Henry Ford began to reveal his intent to create a more public outcome for his growing pile of "true history." In early 1925, the *Detroit Times* reported that Ford planned to build a museum to house "his collection of historical and mechanical specimens that he has been collecting for the past few years." Ford's museum would include transportation, domestic, industrial, and agricultural artifacts—a departure from most other American museums of the time. In fact, only one American museum even remotely resembled the kind of museum Ford wanted to create. In Doylestown, Pennsylvania, Henry Mercer had accumulated a massive collection of everyday objects and with a similar purpose to Ford's—to teach history. In 1923, after a visit to the Mercer Museum, Ford commented, "This is the only museum I've ever been sufficiently interested in to visit. Some day I expect to have a museum which will rival it."

Henry Ford's growing interest in antiques was well known by April 1925 when this cartoon appeared in the *Detroit Times*. Just days before, Ford had launched his own experimental Air Transportation Service to move Ford Motor Company mail and freight by airplane. This cartoon playfully suggested that Ford could also use it to transport his growing number of antiques.

"Perhaps you will be so kind as to aid us in getting together certain information for Mr. Ford's historical records."

So began a "historical questionnaire" that Ford's staff began sending out to "friends 75 years of age and older. . . who are still strong in memory." These questionnaires, which went out in the late 1920s to people who were children before the Civil War, asked questions about the subject's childhood, school life, details of their home, chores, social activities, etc. Many of the questions related to categories of Ford's collecting interests, such as farm equipment, clothing, and lighting methods. Some correspondents sent long, detailed essays, along with daguerreotypes, tintypes, and other old photographs of themselves, something the questionnaire specifically requested. In all, Ford received about 150 responses from all over the country.

"I had known Henry Ford for about twenty minutes, and I was faced with a ten million dollar job—and strange to say, I was not a bit surprised."

– H. F. Morton, *Strange Commissions for Henry Ford*

I. Shown here in a mid-nineteenth-century photograph, this Newcomen engine is the oldest known surviving steam engine in the world.

2. The Newcomen engine installed in the museum. Herbert Morton came to Dearborn to oversee the installation of the English objects he had acquired for Ford.

3. Robert Stephenson's Rocket, built in 1829 for the Liverpool and Manchester Railway in England.

4. Cotswold Cottage on its original site near Chedworth in Gloucestershire, England.

5. The cottage and its adjacent buildings were dismantled and shipped to Dearborn in sixty-seven train cars. The restored cottage, filled with seventeenth-century English antiques, opened in November 1930.

6. Sir John Bennett on its original site on Cheapside in London.

7. In 1931, Ford constructed a two-story version of Bennett's shop in Greenfield Village. Since that time, Greenfield Village's visitors have enjoyed watching the mythological giants Gog and Magog striking the quarter hour.

moving America's Buildings

"If you knew Mr. Ford, why, it didn't matter two hoots what you were doing. If he asked you to do something, why, you would do it."

– Edward L. Cutler, Architect, *Reminiscences*

When Henry Ford walked into the Ford Motor Company drafting office and asked for a man who could handle a job "that was a little out of the ordinary draftsman line of work," Edward J. Cutler quickly found himself thrust into the role of historic preservation architect.

For over two decades, Cutler worked closely with Ford, drawing plans for a "historic village" and seeing to the disassembly and re-erection of buildings in Greenfield Village.

Cutler also designed some village buildings at Ford's request, including a Greek Revival–style Town Hall.

Cutler's travels took him from Massachusetts to Georgia, as he gathered the mills, shops, and homes Ford wanted for Greenfield Village. He carefully sketched and photographed buildings before taking them apart and shipping them to Dearborn. Once the disassembled buildings arrived in the village, crews reassembled them under Cutler's watchful eye. At times, Cutler had only a few weeks to completely dismantle a building, ship it to Dearborn, and rebuild it in the village.

Historic preservation was in its infancy, and Ford and Cutler had no set rules to guide them. Cutler relied on his own knowledge of building design and architecture, photographs and drawings, and Ford's personal, often idiosyncratic, views of how things should look.

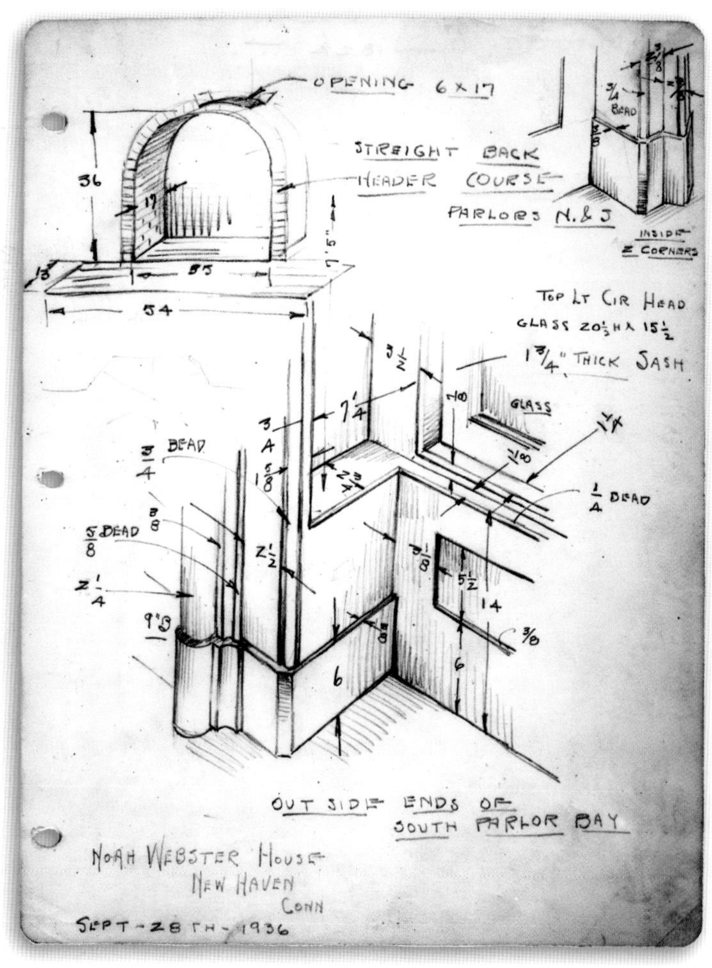

Before dismantling buildings destined for Greenfield Village, Cutler sketched construction details and took careful measurements, such as these sketches of the Noah Webster Home.

(Opposite) Henry Ford appreciated Cutler's ability to sketch any proposed design in detail.

creating Greenfield Village

"Mr. Ford often expressed himself as wanting a village that would be a growing thing, from the early days up to the present."

– Fred Black, Assistant to Henry Ford, *Reminiscences*

Setting his sights on creating Greenfield Village, Henry Ford and his staff had scouted out locations in Dearborn and selected a plot of land with a railroad siding running through it.

Near Fair Lane, Ford's home, and Ford Motor Company's Engineering Building, the land was located near where Ford lived and worked.

Ford created Greenfield Village primarily from buildings that he purchased and moved to the site. He organized the village around a village green with a courthouse, a town hall, a church, a store, an inn, and a school. He placed homes along a road beyond the green. He brought industrial buildings, such as carding mills, sawmills, and gristmills, to the village and made them operate.

Looking eastward, this 1927 aerial view shows the Ford-dominated area where the museum and village would be located. Ford's office was in the Engineering Building.

(Opposite) The general store from Waterford, Michigan, shown here in August 1927, arrived in Greenfield Village in 1928.

The buildings Ford brought to Dearborn to create Greenfield Village fell into four categories: buildings that reflected his life history, buildings associated with Ford's personal heroes, nineteenth-century industrial and civic buildings, and buildings from the region that caught his fancy.

In the summer of 1929, he moved his old schoolhouse, the Scotch Settlement School, which he had preserved in the early 1920s, to join the other historic buildings he was gathering in Greenfield Village. That September, he sat and carved his initials in one of the school desks, just as he had done years earlier as a student.

His memories of trips to a Plymouth, Michigan, carding mill (now Gunsolly Carding Mill) with his father to have raw wool processed led him to buy the 1850s mill, move it to Greenfield Village, and make it operational.

The Clinton Inn was in bad condition when Ford purchased it and moved it to Greenfield Village.

Other regional buildings that Ford acquired for Greenfield Village played no role in his childhood. For example, he bought the 1854 General Store (now the J. R. Jones General Store) from Waterford, Michigan, in 1928. It became the first building brought to the site. The Clinton Inn (now Eagle Tavern) followed shortly after. Ford's agents found the dilapidated 1831 stagecoach inn in Clinton, Michigan, on the Chicago road. As Ford's agents stood inside the crumbling structure, they worried that it might collapse!

To find buildings that belonged to Ford's heroes, his agents traveled across the country.

The most extensive of these pursuits was the re-creation of the Menlo Park Laboratory complex in New Jersey, where Thomas Edison had spent his most prolific years. By this time, the site of the once state-of-the-art lab and its associated buildings had reverted to nature, its empty and abandoned structures scavenged for building materials by

(Above) Martha-Mary Chapel on the village green resembles a New England village church. Bricks and doors from Clara Bryant Ford's girlhood home were used to build the Martha-Mary Chapel.

1. By summer 1929, the restored Clinton Inn (now Eagle Tavern) stood on the village green next to the Waterford General Store (now J. R. Jones General Store).

2. Two of Henry Ford's grandsons posed in front of the building in Smiths Creek, Michigan, before Ford purchased the building and moved it to Greenfield Village. As a boy, Thomas Edison sold newspapers to passengers boarding at stops on the Detroit-to-Port Huron line.

3. Rocks Village Toll House in Greenfield Village in 1929.

4. Phoenixville Post Office in 1930. It was reactivated in Greenfield Village with a new postmark.

5. Ford preserved the Scotch Settlement School on its original Dearborn site in the mid-1920s. In 1929, he moved it to Greenfield Village.

local farmers. Edison had moved his operations to a new facility in West Orange, New Jersey.

In 1928, crews traveled to Menlo Park to document the site after an archeological dig revealed building foundations. Ford's men also negotiated to acquire parts of the original buildings that had been reused in local structures. Reconstruction of the Edison complex began in Dearborn that winter.

FACT:
Ford originally intended his historical village to have residents. Ford aide Jimmy Humberstone and his wife lived for a time in the Sarah Jordan Boarding House, where in May 1929 they welcomed a son, James Jordan Humberstone–the only child ever born in Greenfield Village.

Henry Ford left no detail unattended. He found Edison's old chemical supplier and purchased goods to fill out the shelves. He moved Sarah Jordan's Boarding House, adjacent to Menlo Park, where many of Edison's employees had lived. Agents sought out former employees and collected their reminiscences. Ford's employees worked with Edison and the "Edison Pioneers"—men who had worked with Edison early in his career—to find photos of the original complex. These photographs guided builders to duplicate all the details. Ford had his staff search through Edison's trash and bring back objects found in a refuse pit at Menlo Park, including broken laboratory glassware, pottery shards, and rusted bicycle lamps. Unfortunately, many of these relics dated from the period after Edison left the complex.

Ford's zeal for accuracy was so great, he ordered seven train carloads of New Jersey clay brought to Dearborn to ensure Edison's laboratory

(Below left) The Logan County Courthouse in Postville, Illinois, in 1929, before Ford's crews disassembled it and hustled it to Michigan.

(Below center) Although local citizens cried "foul" and tried to stop the removal, within months of its arrival in Dearborn, the re-erected Logan County Courthouse stood on the village green in 1929.

(Below right) Ford constructed a late nineteenth century-style, steam-powered, working machine shop–Armington and Sims. Ford saw the steam engine as the most visible symbol of America's rise to industrial preeminence.

"Costs never stopped him from doing anything he wanted in the Village. Whenever I'd bring it up . . . he'd always say, 'Did I ever speak to you about cost around here? Did I ever talk to you . . . about something costing too much?'"

- Edward Cutler, *Reminiscences*

To Ford, a steam engine was a thing of beauty, warranting a picture window.

would be reconstructed on New Jersey soil. Ford's construction crew worked through the winter of 1928–29, to ready the complex for the dedication in October 1929.

The representation of Thomas Edison's life in Greenfield Village did not end with the Menlo Park restoration. Ford acquired another building associated with Edison's life in nearby Port Huron, Michigan. As a boy, Thomas Edison had been thrown off a Grand Trunk Western train at a depot in Smiths Creek, Michigan, for accidentally setting fire to the baggage compartment. Ford purchased the building in the spring of 1929 and placed it at the north edge of Greenfield Village near the Michigan Central Railroad tracks.

Ford went to Postville (now Lincoln) in central Illinois to find a building associated with the life of Abraham Lincoln. Ford's purchase of the 1840 Postville courthouse in which Abraham Lincoln had practiced law caused a storm of community protest. Local residents went to court to try to prevent the building from leaving town. Ford's crews had the building disassembled and on its way to Dearborn before the legal proceedings could be completed. Once in the village, the courthouse

went up almost as fast as it had come down. Dismantling had started in Illinois on September 8, 1929. A little more than a month later, the building stood on the village green ready to greet future visitors to Greenfield Village.

Henry Ford admired famed horticulturist Luther Burbank and wanted him represented in Greenfield Village. Burbank's widow gave Ford her husband's 1906 garden office and its contents. The building (now the Luther Burbank Garden Office) had once stood in Burbank's forty-acre experimental gardens in Santa Rosa, California, making it the only western building in Greenfield Village.

Ford added two typical New England buildings to round out his village. The East Haverhill tollhouse (now Rocks Village Toll House) was built in 1828 alongside a Merrimack River drawbridge in Rocks Village, Massachusetts. To fill the time between lifting the drawbridge, several of the toll collectors also worked as cobblers. After it was moved to the village, Henry Ford put a cobbler in the tollhouse to continue the shoe-making tradition.

Ford brought an 1825 post office from Phoenixville, Connecticut, which had served its rural residents through the late nineteenth century. After the building relocated to Greenfield Village, the U.S. Postal Service reactivated it with a Greenfield Village postmark.

Henry Ford memorialized the invention of his first automobile, the 1896 Quadricycle, in a shed behind the home he rented at 58 Bagley Avenue in Detroit. The original shed had been torn down, but Ford used bricks taken from a wall of the Bagley Avenue residence to build a replica of the shed in Greenfield Village in 1933. Inside the reconstructed shed, Ford recreated the workshop where he built the Quadricycle.

ESTABLISHED 1851 — EIMER & AMEND — INCORPORATED 1897
INDUSTRIAL AND EDUCATIONAL
LABORATORY APPARATUS, CHEMICALS & DRUGS
THIRD AVENUE - 18th TO 19th STREET
NEW YORK

LM
DATE OF ORDER 2/22/29
CUSTOMER'S ORDER NO. Ordered by Mr. Jehl
SHIPPED VIA New York Central Railway
SOLD TO Henry Ford, Edison-Menlo Lab., Dearborn, Michigan.
INVOICE DATE 7/31/29
OUR REGISTER NO. 16522
SHIPPED 7/23/29 DN
SHIPPED TO Henry Ford, Edison Menlo Lab., Dearborn, Michigan. Mark For: Experimental Laboratory (upstairs).
APPARATUS DEPARTMENT
TERMS: NET 30 DAYS—PAYABLE IN NEW YORK EXCHANGE

For Case Numbers see Duplicate - Bill

CATALOG NUMBER	QUANTITY	DESCRIPTION	PRICE	PER	EXTENSION
	1/2 lb.	Acetanilid, cryst. usp			
	1 lb.	Acetic anhydride tech.			
	1 pt.	Acetone usp			
	1 pt.	Acetone B.P. 56-57 deg. C cp tp			
	1/4 lb.	Acetphenetidin usp			
	5 lbs.	Acetic acid about 30% tech.			
	500 g.	Acetic acid about 50% cp tp			
	500 g.	Acetic acid glacial 99.1 - 99.5% cp tp			
	5 lbs.	Acid arsenous ~~lump or~~ powd. tech.			
	500 g.	Acid arsenous powd. cp tp			
	500 g.	Acid arsenous cryst. cp			
	1 lb.	Acid benzoic, from toluene usp			
	3 lbs.	Acid boric ~~cryst. or~~ powd. usp			
	500 g.	Acid boric cryst. cp tp			
	1 lb.	Acid boric anhydride fused, whole, pure			
	1 lb.	Acid boric anhydride fused powd. pure			
	25 g.	Acid borotungstic sp.gr. 2.6-3.0 cp			

Cont. on pg. 2

The top photo shows the main laboratory building and brick machine shop under construction in Greenfield Village.

In order to furnish the laboratory as authentically as possible, Ford purchased hundreds of chemicals from Edison's old supplier and filled the walls of the lab with real chemicals.

(Above) Ford spent many nights in the 58 Bagley Avenue shed as he and a group of friends worked on the Quadricycle. The reconstructed shed (pictured here) was one of several buildings in Greenfield Village that reflected Ford's personal history.

In March 1937, Ford dredged a loop of the Rouge River—abandoned when the stream changed course over time—to create a circular Suwanee Lagoon. Still, the Suwanee steamer sat idle much of the time.

The Suwanee steamboat debuted in Greenfield Village in 1935, providing visitors with a boat ride around the Suwanee Lagoon.

FACT:

In addition to the Wright brothers' home and cycle shop, Henry Ford had hoped to acquire their first plane as well, but the Wright Flyer ultimately found a permanent home at the Smithsonian Institution.

Burbank oversaw his experimental gardens from this office. Ford admired the scientific approach that Burbank applied to plant breeding.

Henry Ford and Thomas Edison visited Luther Burbank (center) at his home in Santa Rosa, California, about 1915.

(Right) Ford's meticulous re-creation of the Menlo Park Laboratory in Greenfield Village.

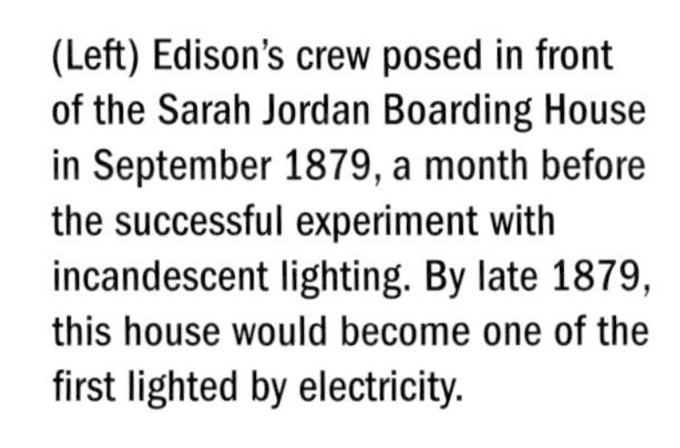

(Left) Edison's crew posed in front of the Sarah Jordan Boarding House in September 1879, a month before the successful experiment with incandescent lighting. By late 1879, this house would become one of the first lighted by electricity.

(Below) The Menlo Park Laboratory is often called the "first modern research laboratory." This large upstairs room was the heart of Edison's "invention factory," the place where Edison and his crew first tested many inventions, including the phonograph and the electric light bulb.

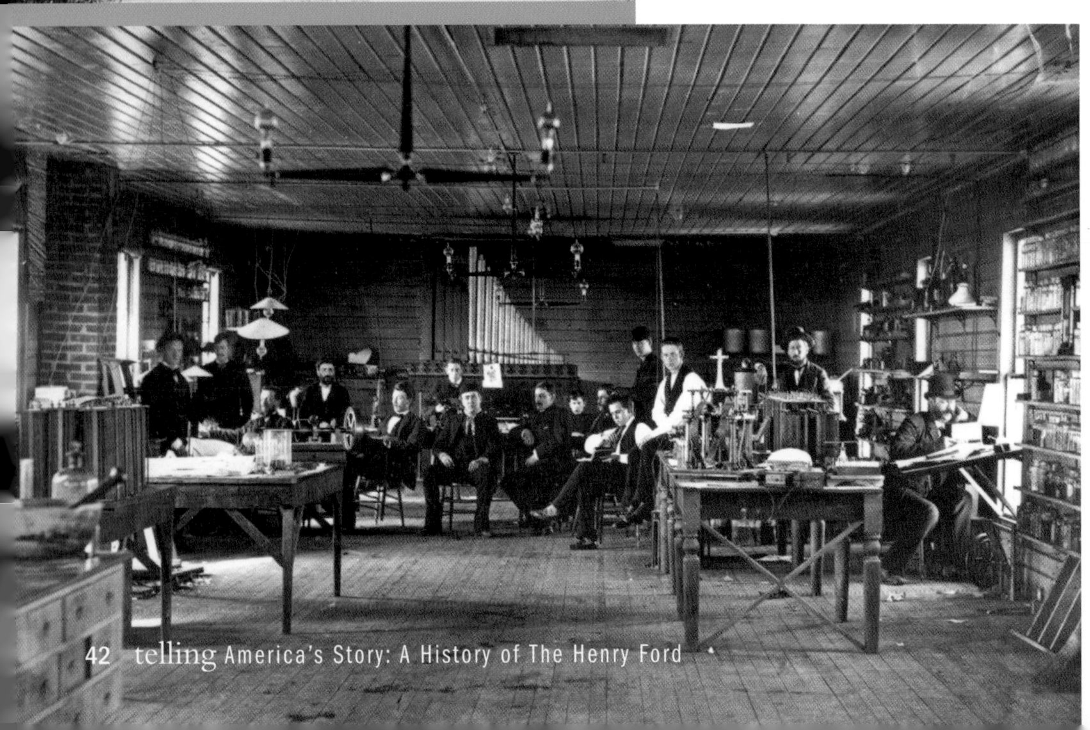

"It's 99.9 percent perfect . . . our floors were never as clean as this."

- Thomas Edison

Mr. Ford

Above are two pieces from a wing of the plane flown at Kitty Hawk, N. C., December 17, 1903.

Orville Wright

Dayton, Ohio,
December 17, 1936.

In 1936, Orville Wright presented Henry Ford with a piece of wood and fabric from the original 1903 Wright Flyer.

The Wright family home in Dayton, Ohio, about 1904, the year after the brothers made their famous flight. The photograph of the Wright brothers' bicycle shop (right) was taken in 1908. The words "Wright Cycle Co." are barely visible above the shop windows.

(Opposite) Henry Ford and Orville Wright on the porch of the Wright home in Dayton, Ohio, in 1936, before Ford had it disassembled and moved to Dearborn.

The original Suwanee boat was a nineteenth-century river steamer that Ford's hero Thomas Edison had frequently ridden during stays at his summer home in Florida. The boat had since sunk, but Ford was able to salvage the engine and installed it on a reconstructed version of the boat.

Ford was a great admirer of Wilbur and Orville Wright, the Dayton, Ohio, brothers who made the first heavier-than-air, powered flight in the world in December 1903. In 1937, Orville Wright assisted in the movement of their family home and bicycle shop from Dayton to Dearborn (his brother Wilbur had died in 1912) and also helped locate many original family possessions, books, machinery, equipment, and tools. The addition of the Wright Home and Cycle Shop was probably the most significant village project of the 1930s. The buildings were dedicated in April 1938, with Orville Wright as the guest of honor.

(Above) Dedication ceremonies for Wright Home and Cycle Shop in April 1938.

Charles Steinmetz was regarded as the greatest electrical engineer of his day. Standing at little more than four feet tall, he overcame a painful spinal deformity to study mathematics and engineering at a German university. He later came to the United States and found work with General Electric Company. He developed ways to make alternating current practical and useful. In 1930, Ford acquired a cabin that Steinmetz used for work and relaxation. The cabin, part of "Camp Mohawk," was originally built in 1896 near Schenectady, New York.

(Left) Charles Steinmetz used this cabin in upstate New York as a retreat where he could work as well as socialize.

"Mr. Ford was aware of the statement that was often made: 'Here is the greatest living industrialist in the manufacture of the most modern means of transportation, who's going back and erecting a monument to the period of the horse and buggy days.' . . . He felt that . . . we could only see the place from which we came by being able to show how things in the past were done."

- Fred Black, *Reminiscences*

(Above) Edsel Ford, George Washington Carver, and Henry Ford stand outside the George Washington Carver Memorial. The interior includes wood from every state in the Union.

(Below) William McGuffey's western Pennsylvania birthplace was a dilapidated log cabin when Ford acquired it.

As a boy, Ford had been strongly influenced by the educational textbooks of William Holmes McGuffey. The McGuffey Readers were among the first objects that Ford collected. Ford located the dilapidated log cabin birthplace of McGuffey in western Pennsylvania, moved it to Dearborn, and rebuilt it. It opened in Greenfield Village in 1934.

Ford learned that the 1823 New Haven, Connecticut, home of Noah Webster was slated for demolition. It was in this home that Webster completed his famous dictionary. Ford purchased the Webster home and had it restored in Greenfield Village, without most of its later Victorian-era additions.

In the 1920s, when traveling by train to Florida, Henry and Clara Ford became acquainted with the area around Ways Station, Georgia, south of Savannah. Ford began purchasing land in the area in 1925 and eventually accumulated about seventy thousand acres, including several old plantations. The Fords built a large, traditional-style home on the Ogeechee River using bricks from The Hermitage, a dilapidated old mansion in Savannah. Starting in 1936, the Fords spent several weeks each year at the home they named Richmond Hill. They became active in many community projects designed to improve the life of local residents. In 1934, they brought two brick slave quarters from Georgia to Greenfield Village. They were placed near the Logan County Courthouse to symbolize enslavement and emancipation.

Ford was a great admirer of the African American agricultural chemist George Washington Carver, whom he honored in both Richmond Hill and Greenfield Village. Although he never directly challenged the Southern system of educational segregation, Ford made significant efforts to improve the schools that served African American children in Richmond Hill. In 1940, he dedicated a new school building as the George Washington Carver School. In 1942, he built the George Washington Carver Memorial in Greenfield Village, modeled on the log house in which Carver was born near the end of the Civil War.

Ford and his chief architect, Ed Cutler, continued to bring small mills and craft operations to the village in the 1930s, further adding to the activity in Greenfield Village. A cooper shop from Kingston, New Hampshire, came to the village in 1932. The 1785 structure was the oldest American craft shop brought to Greenfield Village. As curious

Henry Ford reads by the light of the fire at the restored McGuffey Birthplace in Greenfield Village.

visitors watched, employees fashioned barrels, buckets, and other handmade wooden containers.

Other new industrial buildings included the Hanks Silk Mill and the Tripp Sawmill. The 1810 Hanks Silk Mill from Mansfield, Connecticut, was the first powered silk mill in America. The original wooden silk spinning and reeling machinery had been destroyed by fire, so village craftsmen reproduced it from original patent drawings. Ford even had a mulberry grove planted behind the mill to feed the silkworms he raised for a few years. When the 1855 Tripp up-and-down sawmill from Tipton, Michigan, was installed, it also provided nineteenth-century-style cut lumber for the numerous restoration and construction projects in the village.

Ford added a covered bridge to his village by dismantling the 1832 Ackley Covered Bridge, which spanned a branch of Wheeling Creek in the rolling hills of western Pennsylvania. In 1938, the bridge found new life in Greenfield Village, spanning a small pond.

In 1936, Ford dealers raised money to buy a Cape Cod landmark, a seventeenth-century windmill (now the Farris Windmill), and install

(Right, top to bottom) Webster Home on its original site in New Haven, Connecticut. The home had become a boardinghouse and was scheduled for demolition when Ford acquired it.

Webster Home in Greenfield Village.

The slave homes of the Hermitage Plantation on their original site in Georgia.

This Kingston, New Hampshire, cooper shop, where wooden containers like barrels and buckets were once fashioned by hand, arrived in 1932.

(Far left) Ford's staff brought the 1810 Hanks Silk Mill to Greenfield Village from Mansfield, Connecticut. The Hanks Silk Mill's original wooden silk spinning and reeling machinery had been destroyed by fire, so village craftsmen reproduced it from original patent drawings.

(Left) The 1855 Tripp up-and-down sawmill from Tipton, Michigan.

it in Greenfield Village. When moved to the village, the structure was lifted up on a high stone foundation to provide greater safety and to raise the arms of the working windmill higher into the wind.

The 1851 Richart Wagon Shop from Macon, Michigan, came to the village in the early 1940s. The Richarts used the first-floor room for construction and carpentry work; wagons were hauled up the wooden ramp to the second floor for painting. Along with the building came patterns, parts, tools, family papers, and children's toys from the days when the Richart family built and repaired wagons there.

Susquehanna House was a mid-nineteenth-century tidewater home from St. Mary's County, Maryland, that had once been owned by a slave-owning family. In 1942, when it was offered to Henry Ford, the house was vacant and sitting on land that was to be the site of a new U.S. naval air station. When it was reconstructed in Greenfield Village, its long, wide porches and doors and windows placed across from each other for ventilation represented a decidedly southern regional style, a diversion from the primarily northern-style buildings that populated the village.

When Ford failed to find the buildings he wanted, he had them built. For example, he wanted a chapel but couldn't find one for sale, so he built one and placed it on the village green. He named it Martha-Mary Chapel, after Clara's mother, Martha Bench Bryant, and Henry's mother, Mary Litogot Ford. Henry Ford gave the brand new chapel personal meaning by including a part of his own history in the structure—its

(Below) The Ackley Covered Bridge was dismantled for transport to Dearborn during frigid weather in December 1937. When workmen accidentally dropped a board onto the frozen river, they could easily retrieve it off the ice below.

(Far below) In 1938, the bridge found new life in Greenfield Village, spanning a small pond.

Hundreds of Ford dealers gathered in Dearborn in 1936 for the dedication of the seventeenth century windmill they had presented to Henry Ford.

bricks and doors came from Clara Bryant Ford's childhood home in Greenfield Township, where Henry and Clara were married in 1888.

In 1928, Ford constructed a late-nineteenth-century-style, steam-powered machine shop and named it Armington and Sims after the Providence, Rhode Island, company that built steam engines for Thomas Edison's Pearl Street lighting station in New York City. He placed a picture window on the side of the building so that passersby could watch the Armington and Sims steam engine in action.

The day before the October 21, 1929, dedication celebration, Henry Ford decided he wanted a tintype studio in Greenfield Village. In just one day, Ford's staff built and furnished the studio, and prepared it to operate.

The Soybean Laboratory, which Ford built in Greenfield Village in 1929, represented a view to the future, not the past. Ford built the experimental laboratory to support research into industrial uses for soybeans. During the 1930s, Ford Motor Company chemists conducted their soybean research amidst historic structures, Greenfield Village schoolchildren, and increasing numbers of visitors.

"Pied Piper" Henry Ford leads a group of early American buildings to Greenfield Village in this 1934 cartoon.

The interior of the 1851 Richart Carriage Shop on its original site in Macon, Michigan.

Clara Ford supported her husband in his work at Greenfield Village, but she undertook very few projects of her own. Clara had a fondness for old-fashioned gardens, and the Garden of the Leavened Heart was one of her few village projects. The garden was completed in 1938.

Henry Ford continued adding buildings to Greenfield Village even after it opened to the public in 1933. He continued to locate historic buildings, adding many "pages" to his "animated textbook" during the 1930s and early 1940s. As eager visitors toured the village, craftsmen demonstrated traditional skills, and the sound of schoolchildren added to the hum of activity, additional buildings took their place in Ford's increasingly eclectic village.

Some preservationists questioned the desirability of removing historic buildings from their original sites. And not every building moved to Greenfield Village received the level of attention to accuracy that Ford achieved with the

(Below) When offered to Henry Ford, Susquehanna House was no longer occupied, and was being used to store grain. Ed Cutler, Ford's architect, had to wade through grain eighteen inches deep to take his measurements of the building.

(Below, right) Susquehanna House being re-erected in the village. It was initially furnished as a seventeenth-century home of colonial Maryland.

(Above) An aerial postcard view of Greenfield Village about 1940.

Henry Ford built the soybean laboratory in Greenfield Village in 1929 as a site for research into industrial uses of soybeans.

(Below) The Garden of the Leavened Heart, a project of Clara Ford, was completed in 1938.

Menlo Park buildings. Ford followed his own path, uninfluenced by historic preservation or museum philosophies, and unencumbered by professional standards or scholarship.

Henry Ford continued to select homes, mills, and shops in roughly the same four categories that he had used when he first created the village. Individuals also began to offer Ford historic structures. By the mid-1940s, the village had grown to more than seventy buildings.

henry's Museum, a Panorama of Progress

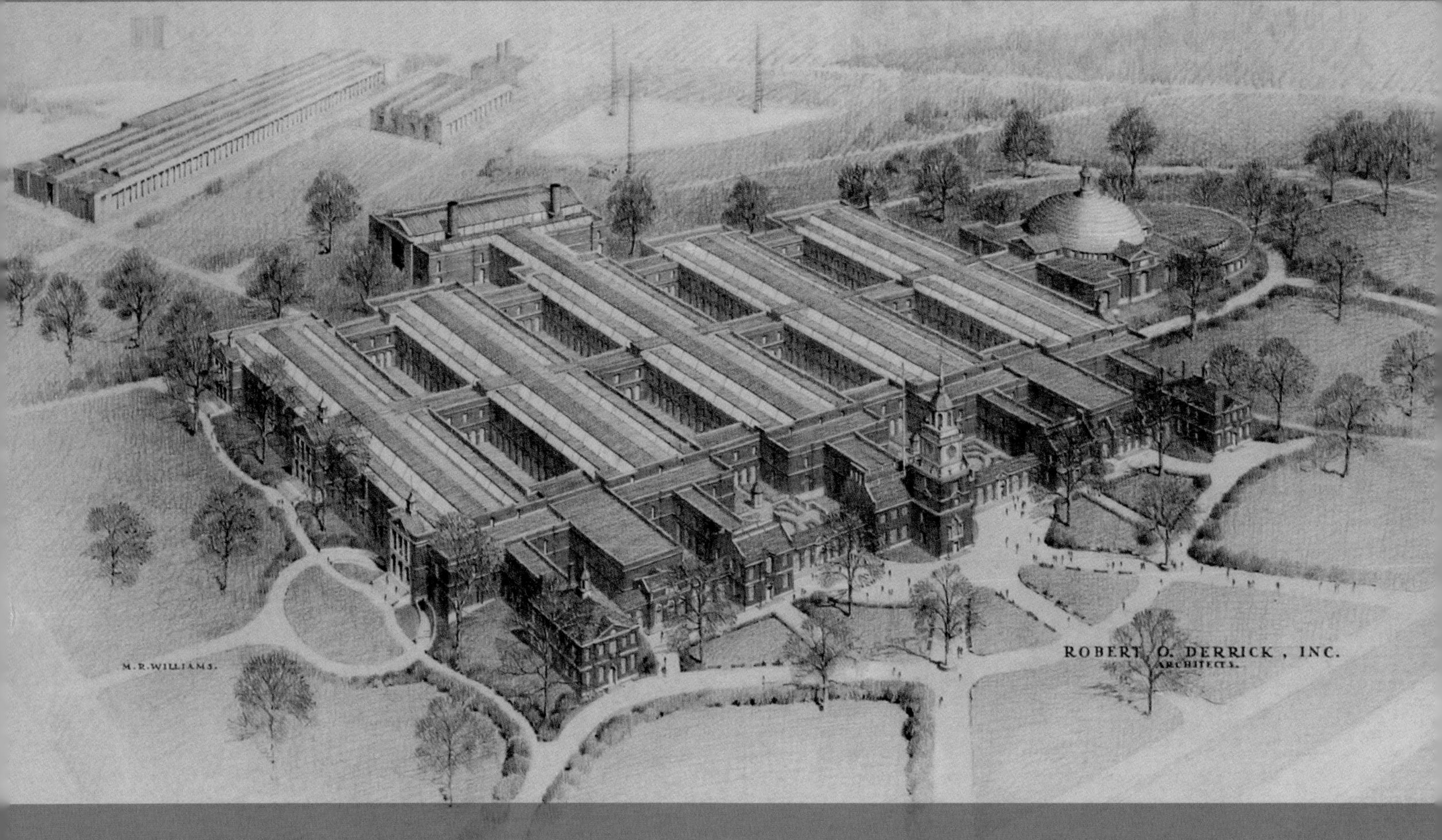

"I found out very soon, of course, that the real director was Henry Ford, who wanted to carry out his own ideas. We planned our exhibits, their interpretation to express his wishes."

– Fred Black, Assistant to Henry Ford, *Reminiscences*

While work on Greenfield Village was underway, architect Robert O. Derrick was designing a large museum building to house Henry Ford's growing collection of Americana.

Derrick suggested that the building façade should resemble Independence Hall and related buildings of Philadelphia, an idea that pleased Ford.

Derrick's original two-story version of his plan included a number of courtyards to break up the massive building, as well as balconies for additional exhibits and basements for storage areas, labs, and workshops. However, Ford saw balconies and basements as places for workers to hide. "I could come in and they wouldn't be working. I wouldn't have it," he commented. Derrick revised his plan accordingly.

After construction began in early spring 1929, the front façade of the building rose quickly, encircling the cornerstone that had been dedicated by Thomas Edison the previous fall. This construction view of the Independence Hall section shows it in August 1929—just a few months before the formal dedication.

(Opposite) Derrick's original plan for Henry Ford's museum included second-floor exhibition areas, which Ford rejected, numerous courtyards, and a domed roundhouse at one end for the display of historic locomotives.

Derrick's final design consisted of a long front façade featuring replicas of Independence Hall, Congress Hall, and Philadelphia's City Hall. The details of the buildings—cornices, pilasters, windows, and arches—mimicked the Philadelphia buildings. The 350,000-square-foot exhibition hall resembled contemporary factory design; its grid of supporting columns placed approximately forty feet apart. The lovely, light-filled front corridors could accommodate the furniture and decorative arts collections. Machinery, vehicles, agricultural equipment, and other substantial objects would be displayed in the large, open area behind the front corridors. Henry Ford's museum would be an interesting combination of elegant Federal-style building in front and practical factory-like space in the rear.

Ford's decision to dedicate his museum on October 21, 1929—the fiftieth anniversary of Edison's invention of the incandescent light bulb—accelerated the pace of construction. In early spring 1929, about

(Above) The museum was not completed at the time of the institution's dedication in October 1929. This aerial view shows the state of construction on the evening of the dedication.

(Right) An abundant display of spinning wheels—without barriers or labels—on exhibit in the museum in 1945.

fifteen acres of Dearborn cornfields were cleared to begin construction of the new museum building. By June 1929, the framing for the front portions of the building was complete. However, the entire building was not finished until the mid-1930s when the teakwood floors were completed.

For several years after the museum officially opened to the public in 1933, visitors found a work in progress. Even as guides took visitors around, workmen completed the eight acres of herringbone pattern teak floor. Arrangements of artifacts were often in flux. Staff used the front corridors to sort glassware and ceramics, while other areas of the museum served as staging areas for creating period room arrangements. Museum guidebooks from the mid-1930s put their best foot forward, advising visitors that "although not yet completed, the museum is being shown to visitors . . . to give them a tour that should prove both fascinating and unique." Museum construction extended well into the 1930s, and the exhibits were not completed until the early 1940s.

What visitors encountered was unlike any other museum experience. The objects ran from the beautiful to the ordinary—from stunning highboys to ordinary plows, spinning wheels, and automobiles. Many of the early steam engines were so large they had to be anchored below ground level.

Henry Ford had rejected the notion of storage rooms, so nearly everything was exhibited on the teakwood floor. Rows of similar objects offered visitors the opportunity

Rows of glassware and ceramics being sorted in the museum's front corridors in 1935.

The early steam engines were anchored into the building's foundation; construction then proceeded around them.

The Street of Shops provided an engaging and nostalgic look at the American past. It was the only display that put objects in context.

(Below) The mock-up of a Colonial kitchen in the back of the museum about 1932.

to observe minute changes in technology and design. If anything, the displays resembled those of an international exposition or world's fair, where appliance or engine or tractor manufacturers proudly displayed their wares. Explanatory labels were few. Ford believed that seeing the physical objects of man's progress had a greater impact than reading about them. In this great grouping of objects, he saw the evolution of technological progress.

FACT:
Henry Ford's son, Edsel Ford, commissioned a replica of the Liberty Bell for the museum's clock tower. The bell was carefully hoisted through the clock opening and then lifted up into the belfry. Henry Ford had instructed his workmen not to let it ring as it was being installed. The inaugural ringing of the Liberty Bell replica was reserved for the dedication ceremonies three weeks later.

A "Street of Shops," built in the 1930s at the suggestion of Edsel Ford, provided a counterpoint to the seemingly endless rows of objects. A series of vignettes represented "old-time" shops such as a toy store, a leather goods shop, and a millinery shop, all filled with objects from Ford's vast collection.

Ford's influence extended to all areas of decision-making. He selected what to keep and what to discard from his piles of stuff. While others might assist with the layout of museum displays, Ford had the final say.

"I was first stationed in the museum where, although the teak floor wasn't even laid, we took visitors around in groups. There were many crated and disassembled machines outside the building in an adjacent field awaiting their turn to be brought in, put in working order and cleaned up."

- Charles E. Smith Jr., *A Home for Our Heritage*, 1979

An Edison Institute high school student offered guests a tour of the museum about 1943. The onset of World War II created a shortage of the young men who had served as village and museum guides. Beginning in 1942, high school and college students attending the Edison Institute Schools were recruited for the guide staff.

Installation of the eight-acre teak floor required a dozen men and went on for several years.

Of all the museum's vast collections, Henry Ford showed the most interest in power-generating and transportation artifacts. The collection of automobiles was among his favorites.

henry's Hero, Thomas Edison

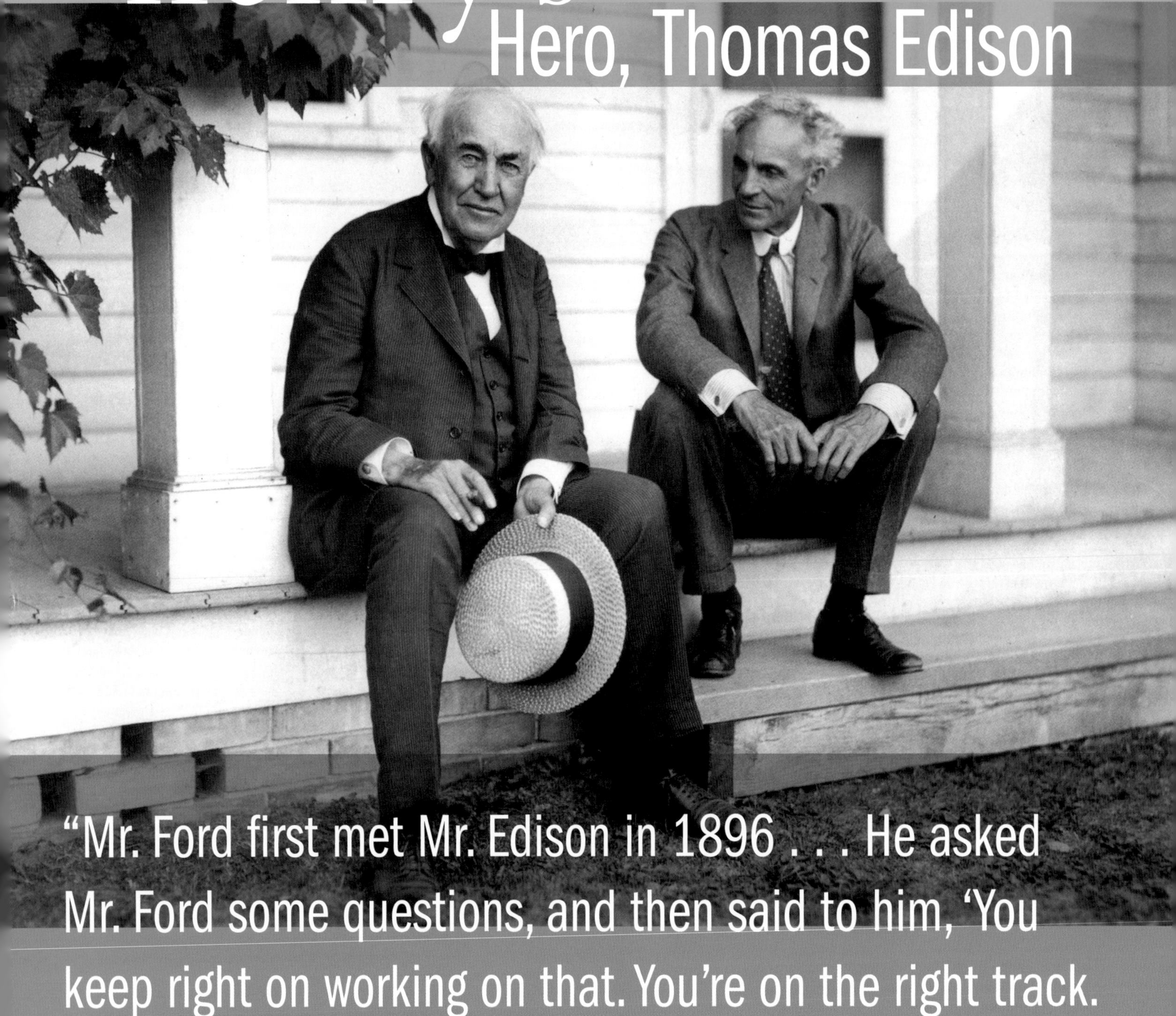

"Mr. Ford first met Mr. Edison in 1896 . . . He asked Mr. Ford some questions, and then said to him, 'You keep right on working on that. You're on the right track. You'll have a power plant that won't be dependent on batteries.' Mr. Ford always said that this was one of the great moments in his life."

– Fred Black, Assistant to Henry Ford, *Reminiscences*

Henry Ford first met Thomas A. Edison at an Edison company convention in New York in 1896.

The great inventor encouraged Ford—then an engineer working at the Edison Illuminating Company plant in Detroit—in his work on an internal combustion engine. Henry Ford never forgot Edison's support and later sought out Edison's friendship after he became famous himself.

When Henry Ford began building his new museum in Dearborn in 1928, Thomas Edison came to dedicate the cornerstone. On September 27, 1928, the then eighty-one-year-old inventor walked carefully across the wet cement, signed his name, and thrust the spade of renowned botanist Luther Burbank into the slab. The cement cornerstone represented Henry Ford's vision of the union of agriculture and industry for the betterment of humanity.

Henry Ford, left, as chief engineer of the Edison Electric Illuminating Company in Detroit.

(Opposite) Edison and Ford, shown here on the porch of Ford's birthplace in 1923, were great friends in their later years.

Henry Ford named the new institution The Edison Institute, in honor of his friend and hero, Thomas Alva Edison.

light's Golden Jubilee

"It seems as if everybody I ever heard of is here."

–Graham McNamee, NBC Broadcaster

On October 21, 1879, Thomas Edison first successfully illuminated his incandescent lamp.

Fifty years later, a number of groups wanted to celebrate the 1929 anniversary in an event to be called "Light's Golden Jubilee."

Edison's former associates, the "Edison Pioneers," were planning an elaborate public festival, but soon realized that they lacked sufficient funding. They approached the General Electric Company, which had absorbed Edison's lamp business, to support a commemorative event. General Electric quickly agreed, seeing the upcoming fiftieth anniversary as a great public relations opportunity. However, no one at General Electric had consulted in advance with Edison about the celebration. Henry Ford convinced Thomas Edison to come instead to Dearborn on October 21, 1929, and use the occasion of Light's Golden Jubilee to dedicate Ford's Dearborn museum as The Edison Institute of Technology. Edward L. Bernays, one of the pioneers of public relations, helped Ford assemble the guest list and handled other details of the event.

The honor of your presence is requested
by
Mr. Henry Ford and Mr. Edsel Ford
at a
Celebration in honor of
Mr. Thomas Alva Edison
on the occasion of
The Fiftieth Anniversary of his
Invention of the Electric Light
and the dedication of
The Edison Institute of Technology
by
The President of the United States
on Monday, October twenty-first
Nineteen hundred and twenty-nine
Dearborn, Michigan

R.S.V.P.

Guests received this invitation to attend the celebration honoring the fiftieth anniversary of the "invention of the electric light" and the dedication of The Edison Institute of Technology by President Herbert Hoover.

The dedication was quite a celebration—with a nationwide broadcast and the attendance of the president of the United States. About three hundred distinguished guests arrived in Dearborn for the event, including Will Rogers, Marie Curie, Orville Wright, Jane Addams, Henry Morgenthau, Walter P. Chrysler, and John D. Rockefeller Jr.

It rained the morning of the dedication ceremonies, but that didn't dampen the enthusiasm of those present. Under a sea of umbrellas and rain slickers, the crowd cheered as President Herbert Hoover, Thomas Edison, and Henry Ford ceremoniously arrived in Greenfield Village for the festivities in a train pulled by an 1850s locomotive.

After the guests had been properly greeted and the press had their quotes and photographs, Henry Ford gave Edison a personal tour of

(Opposite) On the morning of the dedication, hundreds of guests gathered in the rain at Smiths Creek Depot in Greenfield Village to welcome Thomas Edison, President Hoover, and Henry Ford, who arrived in a train pulled by "The President," a wood-burning 1850s locomotive.

Press badge.

(Above) Humorist Will Rogers' breezy response to Ford's invitation to Light's Golden Jubilee.

Henry Ford, President Herbert Hoover, and Thomas Edison walk through the crowds on the rainy October morning.

the Ford Rouge Plant, five miles away. The eighty-two-year-old Edison then retired to Ford's nearby home to rest before the dedication. The guests gathered at the Clinton Inn (now Eagle Tavern) in Greenfield Village for lunch and afternoon horse-drawn carriage tours through the village.

That evening, guests dined in the front corridor of the museum building under elegant crystal chandeliers. To commemorate Light's Golden Jubilee, Ford had the fixtures fitted with tallow candles, hand dipped in Greenfield Village. They were to be extinguished and the museum building lit with electric lights after Edison successfully re-created the lighting of his incandescent lamp in Menlo Park. Unfortunately, the candles burned so quickly the back-up lighting had to be used earlier than planned.

Edison, Ford, and Hoover went to the Menlo Park Laboratory in Greenfield Village, and the inventor went to work re-enacting the lighting of the first electric light bulb. Graham McNamee described the proceedings in a live NBC radio broadcast that reached millions of listeners coast to coast—the nation's first live radio broadcast. As the light bulb began to glow, McNamee

(Above) Dedication day was a miserable, rainy mess. Carriages had to be brought out to transport the guests through the village's muddy streets.

The high point of the evening was Edison's re-enactment of the lighting of his first successful incandescent lamp. During a rehearsal the day before Light's Golden Jubilee, Edison prepared the filament, as Henry Ford and Edison's former assistant Francis Jehl looked on.

FACT:
Edison sat in a wooden chair during the re-enactment in the Menlo Park Laboratory. Ford had the chair nailed to the floor so staff could never move it from its location.

AMERICA'S TRIBUTE TO THOMAS ALVA EDISON BY LEADERS OF INDUSTRY, SCIENCE, LITERATURE, AND ART, ON THE 50th ANNIVERSARY OF HIS INVENTION OF THE INCANDESCENT LAMP

GREENFIELD VILLAGE, DEARBORN, MICHIGAN, OCTOBER 21, 1929

CLASSIFICATION BY NUMBER AND PLACE

1 E. W. STARLING
2 KARL BARTSCH
3 WILLIAM H. ATKINS
4 GEORGE MATTHEW ADAMS
5 JOHN D. ROCKEFELLER, JR
6 MRS. HERBERT C. HOOVER
7 GEORGE EASTMAN
8 JAMES W. GOOD
9 MARIE CURRIE
10 WILLIAM S. BARSTOW
11 MRS. THOMAS A. EDISON
12 EDSEL B. FORD
13 CHARLES EDISON
14 GERARD SWOPE
15 HERBERT C. HOOVER
16 OWEN D. YOUNG
17 HENRY FORD
18 MRS. HENRY FORD
19 THOMAS A. EDISON
20 ANDREW W. ROBERTSON
21 MRS. EDSEL B. FORD
22 ERNEST G. LIEBOLD
23 FREDERICK M. ALGER
24 WILL H. HAYS
25 ROGER M. ANDREWS
26 CHARLES A. EATON
27 THOMAS W. MARTIN
28 ROY D. CHAPIN
29 J. ROBERT LOVEJOY
30 E. E. POTTER
31 WALTER CARY
32 SYDNEY E. BATEMAN
33 B. C. FORBES
34 HARRY M. JEWETT
35 THEODORE BERAN
36 MERLIN H. AYLESWORTH
37 PETER E. MARTIN
38 MERTON E. FARR
39 WALTER P. CHRYSLER
40 CYRUS S. EATON
41 JAMES W. GERARD
42 MRS. WILLIAM B. MELONEY
43 S. B. PAINE
44 PAUL J. KRUESI
45 CHARLES E. SORENSEN
46 WALTER H. THOMPSON
47 HENRY A. HAIGH
48 ROBERT LINDSAY
49 HERMAN PAGE
50 FREDERICK A. SCHEFFLER
51 FREDERICK P. OTT
52 EDGAR B. WHITCOMB
53 MRS. CHARLES EDISON
54 JAMES E. FRASER
55 THEODORE M. EDISON
56 DANIEL C. BEARD
57 ARTHUR H. COMPTON
58 JOHN F. GILCHRIST
59 JOHN B. FORD
60 MRS. WILLIAM CLAY
61 BURCH FORAKER
62 CHARLES G. ABBOTT
63 GEORGE G. BOOTH
64 MRS. THEODORE M. EDISON
65 PATRICK E. CROWLEY
66 JOHN J. O'BRIEN
67 MRS. WILL ROGERS
68 FREDERICK S. STEARNS
69 CAMPBELL B. HODGES
70 LEWIS MILLER
71 ZAY JEFFRIES
72 GRIFFITH OGDEN ELLIS
73 OTTO H. KAHN
74 DEXTER M. FERRY, JR
75 SAMUEL T. DOUGLAS
76 FRED W. GREEN
77 FREDERICK C. FORD
78 WILLIAM J. CAMERON
79 OSSIP GABRILOWITSCH
80 WILL ROGERS
81 C. HAYWARD MURPHY
82 CHARLES C. KELLOGG
83 ALVAN MACAULEY
84 FRANCIS JEHL
85 RICHARD P. JOY
86 PRESTON S. MILLAR
87 ALEX DOW
88 WALTER O. BRIGGS
89 CHARLES H. HODGES
90 EDWARD J. MOINET
91 JOHN G. RUMNEY
92 FRED J. FISHER
93 GILBERT H. GROSVENOR
94 HARRY S. FINKENSTAEDT
95 HENRY SHEARER
96 E. F. W. ALEXANDERSON
97 CHARLES H. MAYO
98 CHARLES B. KING
99 CHARLES W. NASH
100 MRS. CHARLES H. HODGES
101 WM. H. MEADOWCROFT
102 ALLAN SHELDEN
103 HARVEY S. FIRESTONE
104 E. ROY BRYANT
105 JOEL T. BOONE
106 WESSON SEYBURN
107 FREDERICK W. HODGES
108 MRS. H. S. FIRESTONE
109 SAMUEL INSULL
110 GORDON S. RENTSCHLER
111 JOHN J. CARTY
112 WILLIAM E. SCRIPPS
113 HENRY MORGENTHAU
114 MICHAEL J. MURPHY
115 HENRY V. A. PARSELL
116 WALLACE R. CAMPBELL
117 MRS. JOHN EYRE SLOANE
118 H. P. LIVERSIDGE
119 ERNEST C. KANZLER
120 GEORGE M. REYNOLDS
121 FIELDING H. YOST
122 HOWARD E. COFFIN
123 GEORGE C. OSBORN
124 HENRY B. JOY
125 ALBERT KAHN
126 BEN B. LINDSEY
127 MRS. ERNEST C. KANZLER
128 GEORGE H. BARBOUR
129 MARSHALL E. SAMPSELL
130 CHARLES B. WARREN
131 WILLIAM B. MAYO
132 RICHARD H. WEBBER
133 EDWARD C. ELLIOTT
134 JULIUS ROSENWALD
135 EDWARD B. MILLER
136 HARRY H. BENNETT
137 MARTIN P. RICE
138 MAURICE CASTEL
139 CHARLES L. CLARKE
140 ORVILLE WRIGHT
141 JOHN EYRE SLOANE
142 FREDERICK F. SMITH
143 WILLIAM H. EASTON
144 MELVIN H. SIPPLE
145 WILLIAM H. MacKAY
146 A. E. ALLEN
147 FRANK W. HUBBARD
148 DANIEL WILLARD
149 IRVING R. BACON
150 F. C. FOSTER
151 CHARLES DANA GIBSON
152 MRS. EDWARD B. MILLER
153 BENJAMIN B. LOVETT
154 FREDERICK D. POTTER
155 JOHN C. SHAFFER
156 JOSEPH BOYER
157 THEODORE W. FRECH
158 WILLIAM W. NICHOLS
159 CLARENCE M. BURTON
160 WALTER H. MILLER
161 ADOLPH S. OCHS
162 RANSOM E. OLDS
163 MRS. FRANK A. POTTER
164 R. MUSHA
165 LEE DeFOREST
166 FRANK J. SLADEN
167 J. ROBERT CROUSE
168 JULIUS H. HAASS
169 CHARLES F. BURGESS
170 H. M. DOUBLEDAY
171 ROBERT H. TANNAHILL
172 ALFRED O. TATE
173 ROY D. McCLURE
174 MURRAY W. SALES
175 ALEXANDER G. RUTHVEN
176 WILLIAM J. GRAY
177 FRANK CAMPSALL
178 FRANK P. BOOK
179 ALBERT S. HOWE
180 PAUL D. CRAVATH
181 D. STAIR
182 GEORGE W. CATO
183 FRANK W. SMITH
184 ALBERT R. ERSKINE
185 HARRY REID
186 HENRY E. BODMAN
187 CHARLES M. SCHWAB
188 CLARENCE H. BOOTH
189 R. H. UNDERWOOD
190 JOSEPH F. PORTER
191 W. WINANS FREEMAN
192 C. HERRICK HAMMOND
193 RALPH H. BOOTH
194 WILLIAM J. HAMMER
195 JOHN W. SCHROEDER
196 ROBERT H. CLANCY
197 HIRAM H. WALKER
198 SAMUEL W. STRATTON
199 FRANK A. KETCHAM
200 WILLIAM T. BARBOUR
201 EDWIN W. RICE, JR
202 PRESTON S. ARKWRIGHT
203 AUGUST EIMER
204 CHALRES L. EDGAR
205 JOHN TRIX
206 JOHN G. BARRY
207 WILMER R. VALENTINER
208 JOHN V. MILLER
209 FELIX J. C. POLE
210 N. G. SYMONDS
211 EDWIN S. WEBSTER
212 JOHN G. LEARNED
213 B. G. TREMAINE
214 ALBERT A. ALBRECHT
215 JAMES T. WHITEHEAD
216 SYLVESTER R. WAY
217 WILLIAM H. ONKEN, JR
218 RAYMOND C. DAHLINGER
219 CHALRES A. STONE
220 MRS. JOHN V. MILLER
221 WILLIAM GREEN
222 HENRY D. SHUTE
223 JERE C. HUTCHINS
224 W. H. TAYLOR
225 H. FREEMAN BARNES
226 GOERGE E. CULLINAN
227 BURT J. CRAIG
228 WILSON W. BACHANAN
229 McPHERSON BROWNING
230 HERMANN LEMP
231 THOMAS N. McCARTER
232 MRS. ORLA B. TAYLOR
233 JANE ADDAMS
234 GEORGE F. MORRISON
235 ORLA B. TAYLOR
236 SIDNEY T. MILLER
237 ATWOOD M. FISHER
238 JOHN BARRAN
239 ALEXANDER MUNGLE
240 NAP H. BOYNTON
241 FRANK C. BARR
242 PAUL A. SCHOE
243 RUSSELL DOUB
244 JOHN EDISON S
245 ERNEST J. BERG
246 CHALRES L. O'D
247 LOUIS H. EGAN
248 CHARLES W. JE
249 GEORGE F. PEAB
250 JAMES E. DAVID
251 W. O. BATCHEL
252 WILLIAM M. HA
253 MRS. MATTHEW
254 MATTHEW S. S
255 WILLIAM M. BR
256 P. B. SHAW
257 HERBERT B. FLO
258 SARAH M. SHER
259 BENSON FORD
260 SAMUEL E. DOA
261 WILLIAM FORD
262 HENRY FORD, II

announced excitedly, "It lights! Light's Golden Jubilee has come to a triumphant climax!" Car horns sounded; lights flashed on and off. The bell in the museum clock tower rang, and a plane flew by with "Edison" and "79" and "29" illuminated under the wings. The world bathed itself in electric light in tribute to Edison.

After completing the reenactment, Edison, Ford, and Hoover returned to the museum and heard accolades from Madame Curie and President Hoover, and even Albert Einstein—by way of a radio address from Germany—praising Edison for his contributions to the world. Edison himself walked up to the microphone and, with his voice breaking with emotion, briefly thanked the crowd. Henry Ford did not address the crowd at all—he simply basked in the well-deserved recognition given to his friend and mentor Edison.

Henry Ford had succeeded in "kidnapping" Light's Golden Jubilee away from General Electric and had made it his own. Ford's new museum complex, formally named The Edison Institute in honor of Thomas Edison, was properly christened, with dignitaries from all over the country paying homage to his hero.

There were no photographs taken of the Light's Golden Jubilee banquet, so this painting of the event was created after the fact. In the mid-1930s, Henry Ford asked his staff artist, Irving Bacon, to capture the event in a panoramic painting, which took nearly a decade to complete.

(Opposite) This line drawing identified all of the notables who were present at the Light's Golden Jubilee banquet.

As part of the national celebration, the United States Postal Service marked the occasion of Light's Golden Jubilee by issuing a commemorative stamp.

Program for Light's Golden Jubilee.

PROGRAM

The Hon. Owen D. Young, *Toastmaster*

Introductory Address

THE HON. OWEN D. YOUNG

Arrival of Mr. Edison at his Menlo Park laboratory

Re-enactment of his invention of the electric lamp

Tribute of the Pioneers

MR. WILLIAM SLOCUM BARSTOW
President of the Edison Pioneers

Remarks

PROF. ALBERT EINSTEIN
Speaking from Berlin, Germany

MR. THOMAS ALVA EDISON

MR. HENRY FORD

Dedication of the Edison Institute of Technology

THE HON. HERBERT C. HOOVER
President of the United States

As Mr. Edison's re-enactment of his invention will take place in the laboratory building, which can accommodate only a small group, it necessarily must be beyond the vision of the dinner guests. Amplifiers will bring a description of the ceremony to the banquet room. Guests are requested to remain at their tables for the return of the President and the completion of the evening's events with the President's address.

Sharing a Founder

Henry Ford founded the Ford Motor Company in 1903. Twenty-six years later, he incorporated The Edison Institute as a private, nonprofit educational organization. The museum and village were never a part of Ford Motor Company, although many people mistakenly believed that they were. During Henry's lifetime, the line between the company and The Edison Institute was often blurry. In his early days of collecting, Henry stored his acquisitions in company buildings, and he often deployed company employees—from managers to trades people—to work on projects for the museum and village. Moreover, the museum and the village are bordered on all sides by company property and buildings. This confusion still lingers.

A replica of Edison's 1879 carbon filament light bulb made at the Menlo Park Lab and presented to Henry Ford by Thomas Edison two days before Light's Golden Jubilee.

“learn to Do by Doing”

“Learn to do by doing—that’s my favorite principle in education.”

– Henry Ford, *Good Housekeeping*, October 1934

Henry Ford's primary interest in creating the museum and village was to provide for the education of America's youth.

Greenfield Village opened as a campus for the private Edison Institute Schools in September 1929. Thirty-two students began classes at Scotch Settlement School, launching Henry Ford's unique educational vision, which combined progressive education, nineteenth-century traditional schooling, and "learning by doing."

By the late 1930s, Ford's schools had grown to nearly two hundred students, ranging from kindergarten through high school. Many of the students at the Edison Institute Schools were related to Ford Motor Company managerial employees, and nearly all of them came from Dearborn. Numerous village buildings and areas in the museum became classrooms for the growing student body that graduated its first high school class in 1937.

Ford gave the students free run of the village and museum. Even after the village formally opened to the public, Henry Ford made it clear that, despite the presence of paying guests, there was no place off limits to the schoolchildren. The staff was instructed not to let the visiting public interfere with the ability of the students to enjoy and learn from their surroundings.

Ford's philosophy of education was "learn to do by doing." It was a way of learning that Ford had experienced during his own childhood, and the way, in fact, that he himself learned best. Ford was committed to "functional education" that gave young people experiences with ways of making a living. In Henry Ford's Edison Institute Schools, students would learn not only from books, but also from objects and experiences.

Students were taught using both traditional and progressive methods. Standard academic subjects like reading, arithmetic, geography, and science were at the core of their studies. Pupils used the artifacts and many of the historic buildings in the village for practical learning. Girls practiced housekeeping skills while boys got experience in a machine shop. As more students enrolled, more village buildings accommodated

Scotch Settlement schoolchildren lined up on the Edison Institute School's first day of operations on September 16, 1929. Ford put four grades in the one-room school—just as it would have been fifty years earlier.

(Opposite) A photographer caught these students at their lessons at the Secretary Pearson House (now Giddings Family Home) in 1944.

THE proceeds of your share in the Greenfield Village and Edison Institute Roadside Market last season are inclosed. This is the amount realized from the sale of vegetables from the school gardens this year after you had taken home all you wished. There were some expenses to be deducted, such as the cost of labor and the cost of selling. There remains the total sum of $4100.00. Divided among our 163 pupils, this amounts to $25.15 each. In presenting you with your share, we express the hope that you will find next year's gardening still more enjoyable and profitable.

(Above) Students operated a produce stand at the intersection of Village and Southfield roads.

Edison Institute high school boys learned to fix Model T's.

classes. Reflecting Ford's interest in balancing urban and rural experiences, each pupil worked a vegetable plot in the village. Students even operated a produce market at the intersection of Southfield and Village roads. Each student who worked a vegetable garden plot in the village received a portion of the profits, often earning $25 a year per student.

The younger children made the village their playground—jumping rope, roller skating, and sledding among the historic buildings. Students also enjoyed an amazing array of other activities, offering an outlet for whatever talents and interests they possessed. They researched and wrote articles for the school newspaper, acted in plays, learned to ride horses, played on the basketball team, wove textiles, made pottery, and operated a radio station. Students often had the opportunity to meet famous people who came to tour the museum, such as Mickey Rooney and Walt Disney, who both visited in the 1940s.

The Edison Institute Schools fielded sports teams and offered a full range of physical activities. The Recreation Building (now Lovett Hall), designed by museum architect Robert O. Derrick and completed in 1937, provided facilities for the

The Edison Institute "Volts" baseball team posed for a team photo in June 1936.

(Left) Pupils, dressed in nineteenth-century clothing, re-enacted Lincoln court trials in the Logan County Courthouse.

FACT:

Ford supplied everything, from school supplies to bus transportation to lunches. He charged no tuition to attend Edison Institute Schools.

In this 1940 photograph, students pose in Tom Thumb's carriage with movie star Mickey Rooney, one of America's most popular actors at the time.

(Below) Walt Disney taught a student to draw Mickey Mouse during his 1940 visit to the museum.

growing school system. The building housed a gymnasium, squash courts, swimming pool, library, and a ballroom, the site of student dances. Ford made sure that the students had the opportunity to learn the contra dances of which he was so fond.

Not surprisingly, Ford had the beloved McGuffey Readers of his youth reprinted so that the children in his Edison Institute Schools could use them. Like Ford, children had found the readers great fun as well as instructive, and they tended to remember the verses and stories contained in the readers. The books taught children traditional values like industry, kindness, and virtue, as well as reading and writing. McGuffey Readers had a deep and lasting influence on Henry Ford, and he wanted to share them with the new generation of children attending his Edison Institute Schools.

Lovett Hall under construction. The building eventually housed a gymnasium, squash courts, swimming pool, library, and a ballroom.

(Below) Benjamin Lovett, Henry Ford's dance instructor, conducts a dance class in the Lovett Hall ballroom (named for Benjamin Lovett).

a working Village

"Mr. Ford dislikes mere 'dead' exhibitions of things; he wishes to see them in action."

– Frank Campsall, Secretary to Henry Ford, *Reminiscences*

The publicity arising from the October 1929 dedication event, as well as the numerous articles published in national magazines and newspapers, intensified public interest in Henry Ford's historical venture.

Ford's aggressive acquisition and restoration activities had piqued the public's curiosity. They wanted to see the results of all this for themselves.

But Henry Ford was in no hurry to let the public in to the museum or the village. Since there were no provisions for visitors, each request required the staff's consideration and decision. Some visitors might be turned away from Greenfield Village, while others received a personal tour. Visitors requesting a visit to the museum had to apply to receive a special pass.

By 1932, it was evident that formal arrangements needed to be made to accommodate an eager public. Construction began on a colonial-style waiting room, known as the Gatehouse (now the Ticket Building), which would serve as the visitors' entrance to Greenfield Village. The first formal public visitors were admitted on June 22, 1933. About a week later, the museum welcomed its first official visitors, even though the facility was still under construction.

These early visitors enjoyed a Greenfield Village that was filled with activity. Thirty-one full-time craftsmen wove and knitted goods, took tintype photographs of visitors, made shoes, created pottery, produced barrels, ground grain into flour, fashioned objects out of molten glass, and worked as blacksmiths—all in full view of visitors. Students from the Edison Institute Schools often worked alongside experienced craftsmen. Many of the handcrafted products were then offered for sale in the village shops. Handmade nails and horseshoe paperweights made by the blacksmiths were particularly popular souvenirs in the 1930s.

This map showed Greenfield Village as it looked when it officially opened to the public in June 1933.

(Opposite) The Village Gatehouse (now Ticket Building), completed in May 1933, served as the formal entrance to Greenfield Village.

(Above) Famed landscape architect Jens Jensen created a plan for landscaping Greenfield Village in 1935. Twenty years earlier, Jensen had transformed the farmland around Henry Ford's Fair Lane estate into a panorama of ornamental trees, sweeping meadows, and elegant gardens. Jensen worked with naturalist John Burroughs on the Fair Lane landscape to incorporate a wildlife refuge for deer, foxes, woodchucks, and many species of birds. Though Jensen's plan for Greenfield Village was never completely implemented, he left a lasting influence on the property.

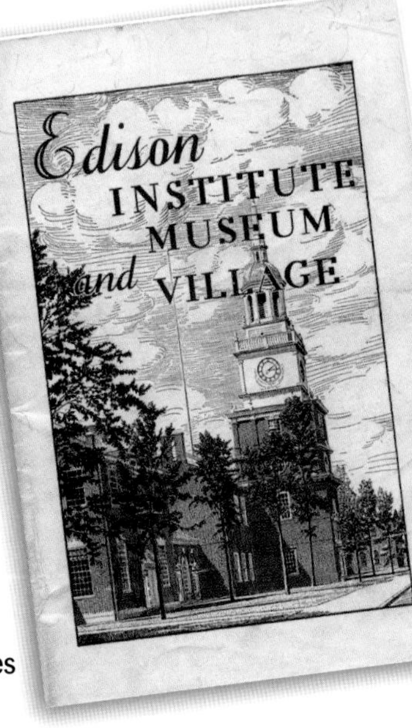

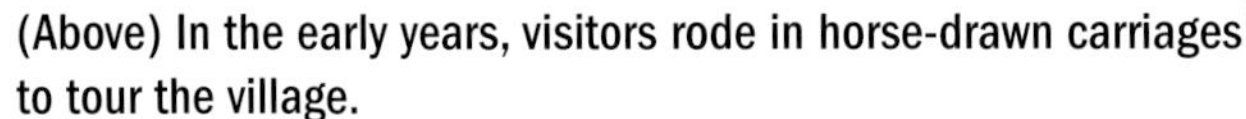

(Above) In the early years, visitors rode in horse-drawn carriages to tour the village.

(Right) This guidebook, published about 1940, advertised handicrafts and publications produced on premises.

Other village craftsmen worked to support Ford's restoration efforts. Brickmakers and sawyers operated nineteenth-century equipment to produce authentic period bricks and lumber that could be used in village restoration and construction projects. Blacksmiths fashioned hardware and implements for use in village buildings. Flour and meal ground at the Loranger Gristmill were used in Edison Institute School student lunches and packaged for sale to the public.

Ford's staff had to hustle to stay one step ahead of the new challenges created by the growing number of visitors. New carriages were readied for group tours. Snack stands sprang up, and guidebooks were

(Left) Henry Ford used to grab a fast meal at this lunch wagon, called the Owl Night Lunch, when he worked the night shift in Detroit during the 1890s. In the early years of Greenfield Village, the Owl Night Lunch offered the only food service to visitors, serving hamburgers, frankfurters, coffee, milk, and soda.

(Below) Across the road from the museum clock tower, workers completed a new parking lot in 1936. Before the lot was completed, visitors parked everywhere.

FACT:
By the late 1930s, products of the Greenfield Village craft shops were being shipped all over the United States and as far away as India and South America.

printed for purchase. Daily summer visitation approached one thousand a day in the mid-1930s and included royalty, Hollywood stars, and American industrialists. Annual attendance reached over five hundred thousand paid admissions by the late 1930s.

(Top left) Photographer Charles Tremear demonstrated the nineteenth-century process of tintype photography in the Greenfield Village Tintype Studio.

By the late 1930s, thousands of visitors were stopping by the Tintype Studio each year to have their portraits made, including celebrity visitors such as Joe Louis (far above) and Walt Disney (above).

FACT:
Initially, adult visitors paid twenty-five cents admission, while children entered for ten cents. School groups were admitted free. Henry Ford made no real effort to profit from admissions or sales of souvenir postcards and craft items. In the first years, each visitor cost the institution about five dollars.

(Above left) The wedding of Arthur and Eileen Lamminen in June 1935, pictured here, was the first wedding to take place in Martha-Mary Chapel. Since then, thousands of couples have taken their vows there.

(Above center) Students weave in the Plymouth Carding Mill (now Gunsolly Carding Mill). Some of the best works of these students were sold or put on display.

(Above right) Shown here in 1932, glassblowers in the Menlo Park complex crafted incandescent light bulbs like those created for Thomas Edison in 1879.

(Left) In the Loranger Gristmill, two stone grinding wheels turned out one barrel of wheat flour or corn meal an hour.

a place of Solace and Refuge

"[Visiting] my office and work in the village were safety valves for the pressure and strain of the Ford Motor Company . . . [Ford] spent so much time around the village . . . It was a relief for him to get down there."

– Edward Cutler, Architect, *Reminiscences*

Greenfield Village was a tonic to Henry Ford.

He reveled in the whirr of steam engines and the sound of children's voices in song at the Martha-Mary Chapel. The bucolic village was more than a refuge for Ford—it represented the small-town life that he hoped Americans might return to some day, moving from congested cities back to farms in which one might be more independent. The village reminded him of an American past that he and the Model T had changed forever.

(Opposite) Henry and Clara Ford, shown here in the late 1930s, enjoyed strolling through Greenfield Village whenever they could.

The Edison Institute schoolchildren's antics and activities were a source of great joy for Clara and Henry Ford. One assistant remarked that Ford knew more about school operations than the operations of Ford Motor Company during the 1930s.

(Right) Ford loved tinkering with timepieces and set up watch repair benches everywhere—in Ford Birthplace, at his home, and in jewelry shops in Greenfield Village, such as this one in Magill Jewelry Shop (now Cohen Millinery), where Ford worked on a watch in the 1940s.

FACT:

When Henry Ford moved his birthplace to Greenfield Village, he had bushes planted to hide a path that allowed him to enter the house without being seen.

The Detroit News Pictorial Magazine, April 5, 1953

(Above) By the 1940s, the city of Dearborn was growing up around the Ford family homestead, and the house required twenty-four-hour security protection. In January 1944, Henry Ford's birthplace was cut in two and hauled by truck a few miles from the Dearborn farmstead to its new location in Greenfield Village.

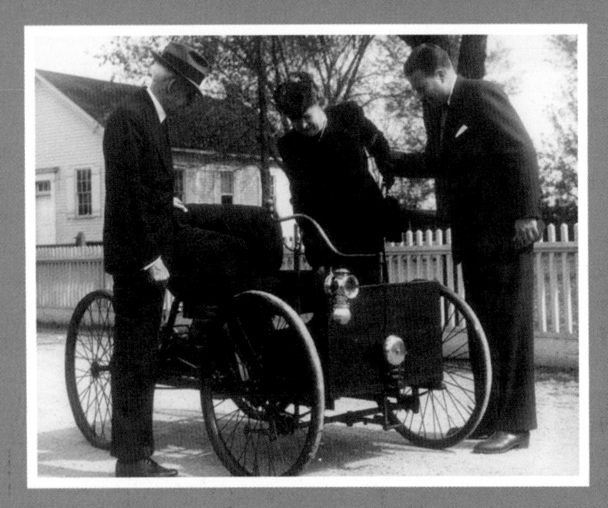

In May 1946, assisted by grandson Henry II and accompanied by his wife Clara, Ford took a spin through the village in the Quadricycle.

In 1945, Henry Ford added one last building to the village, a one-quarter-scale reproduction of his first automobile factory, the Ford Motor Company Mack Avenue plant.

The 1940s were quieter years for the museum and village. As World War II tooled up, activities and personnel were cut back, not as many visitors attended, and the Edison Institute school system was reduced in size.

Although Ford added few new buildings, he rounded out the representation of his personal history with replicas of the one-room Miller School he attended, the Edison Illuminating Company power plant in Detroit where he worked, and the Mack Avenue Automobile Plant, his first automotive plant (these last two at reduced scale). In 1944, Ford moved his childhood home—which he had so painstakingly preserved on the family farm twenty-five years before—to Greenfield Village, assuring that it would be cared for after he was gone.

(Above) Clara Ford, accompanied by Mrs. Gaston Plantiff, Mrs. Grace Prunk, and Harvey Wismer, walks into Lovett Hall.

(Below) More than one hundred thousand people filed past the Village Gatehouse on their way to the first floor lobby of Lovett Hall to pay their respects to Henry Ford as he lay in state.

Full Story of Ford's Life on Page 4; Pictures Page 5

WARMER
The Detroit Free Press
SECOND METRO FINAL
EXTRA
TUESDAY, APRIL 8, 1947
On Guard for Over a Century
Vol. 116—No. 339
Five Cents

HENRY FORD DIES

Succumbs Quietly at 83 with Wife at His Bedside

Henry Ford, founder and builder of the vast Ford industrial empire, died at 11:40 p. m. Monday at his residence in Dearborn. He was 83 years old.

The venerable pioneer of the automobile industry, who pumped life's blood into the economic system of Detroit and the Nation, would have celebrated his 84th birthday July 30.

His death came very suddenly and the cause was not announced immediately. Ford had been very active over the week-end, members of his family said.

Ford, in a simply phrased letter of resignation had stepped down for the second time as active monarch of his empire on Sept. 21, 1945.

* * *

EARLIER, he had relinquished the management to his only child, Edsel, but when Edse' died on May 26, 1943, he took over the reins again for two years and three months.

Then he surrendered the presidency of the Ford Motor Co. to his grandson, Henry Ford II. At that time, the elder Ford was in excellent health, but he wanted to devote more time to personal interests.

In recent months, however, his health began to fail and his public appearances became less frequent, although he enjoyed his periods of outside activity.

* * *

HE HAD BEEN able to spend some time each week at the Ford engineering laboratory where he maintained a private office and workshop, but was rarely seen about the administration building where affairs of the big company were directed.

His last formal public appearance was a week before Christmas, when he presented watches to veteran employees of his company. At the end of a bleak and cold February, Ford journeyed to his home in Richmond Hills, Ga., where he rested and sought to recapture his vitality.

He returned to Dearborn just eight days ago.

Mr. Ford's wife was the only one with him when he died.

His death was announced 90 minutes later by the Ford News Bureau, which arranged a telephone hook-up with all of Detroit's newspapers and the various wire services.

* * *

ALL OF THE immediate family are in Detroit, with the exception of one grandchild, Benson Ford. Benson was rushing back from New York, where he had been on a business trip.

The other grandchildren, in addition to Henry Ford II, are William Ford and Mrs. Walter Buhl Ford II.

Ford's death started immediate speculation as to the probable disposition of his vast personal fortune, which like that of his late son, Edsel, has been estimated variously at upward of $200,000,000.

It was generally assumed, in the absence of any statement from the family, that all of the elder Ford's holdings probably would go directly to his widow, Mrs. Clara Bryant Ford.

With Mrs. Ford, the founder of the great Ford empire owned approximately 58 per cent cent of the voting stock of the giant enterprise.

The remaining 42 per cent was understood to be held by Edsel Ford's heirs, Mrs. Eleanor Clay Ford, his widow, her three sons, Henry II, Benson and William and her daughter, Josephine.

* * *

A LARGE PART of the Ford stock, however, was in nonvoting shares, and was held by the Ford Foundation, founded by the elder Ford more than a decade ago to promote educational interests. As such it was tax exempt.

When Edsel Ford died in 1943 it was said the inheritance tax would eat up a large part of his estate. There even was speculation that to satisfy the tax, some of the Ford stock would have to be sold outside the Ford family.

The difficulty arose immediately of determining the exact value of a share of Ford Motor Co. stock, however. So far as has been disclosed, probate of his estate has not yet been completed.

Presumably the same problem will arise in attempting to determine the exact monetary value of the elder Ford's holdings in the company.

As far as the great Ford industrial empire is concerned, however, it will go on as usual, with the second Henry Ford and nearly a dozen vice presidents directing its destinies.

1863 — 1947

Free Press Photo

HENRY FORD
His memory will live forever in Detroit

U.S. Plan on Greece Blasted by Gromyko

BY JAMES E. ROPER

LAKE SUCCESS, N. Y.—(UP)—Russia attacked American plans to send direct aid to Greece and Turkey.

The Russian spokesman demanded that the United Nations administer any American help sent to Greece.

Soviet Delegate Andrei Gromyko asked the UN Security Council to set up a special commission to make sure that any help offered Greece was used only for the benefit of the Greek people.

He charged that President Truman's program, as originally proposed, was "political."

It deals "a serious blow" to the UN and "produces distrust" among UN members, Gromyko said.

President Truman has proposed to spend $250,000,000 to help Greece and $150,000,000 to help Turkey.

The program would include both military and economic aid and would be carried out independently of UN.

Gromyko charged the plan was inconsistent with UN's "purposes and principles" the maintenance of peace. He said it would intensify the Greek civil war.

* * *

GROMYKO'S proposal for UN supervision of Greek aid apparently was intended to prevent the United States from offering mili-

Turn to Page 3, Column 4

TOWN'S DILEMMA

Lights Voted: Pay Refused

Center Line voters Monday expressed a desire to have darkened city streets relighted, but disapproved raising taxes to pay for it.

The proposal to end the blackout was approved by a vote of 336 to 106, but the accompanying proposal to raise the tax limit two mills was beaten, 209 to 199.

The lights on Center Line's side streets were turned off during the early 1930s as an economy measure. A proposal to light them again was voted down several years ago.

Paraguay Chief Rejects Mediation

ASUNCION, Paraguay (UP)—President Higinio Morinigo and ...

Wallace Denies Political Ambition

NEW YORK (UP)—Henry A. Wallace said before leaving for Europe by plane that he had "no political ambitions whatever."

Wallace said he planned to visit London, Stockholm and Paris and ...

Local Issues Fail to Lure Suburb Vote

Floods Blamed for Vacant Polls

Despite contests for municipal offices and balloting on local issues, voting was generally light in suburban communities in the Detroit area Monday.

Highland Park, some downriver towns and communities in Southern Oakland and Macomb Counties were choosing city officials.

In some of the areas where moderately heavy balloting was expected flood conditions were blamed for keeping voters away from the polls.

Ferndale

Ferndale voters ousted two members of the City Commission in the lightest vote in a spring election since 1931.

The two new commissioners are Sidney G. Hill, president of the Ferndale Labor Club, and Murray A. Scott, a personnel official of the Packard Motor Car Co. They defeated Commissioners George J. Kling and Hugh R. Liddicoat.

The vote was: Hill, 1,473; Scott, 1,119; Kline, 834; Liddicoat, 753.

The two present constables were re-elected. The vote: Robert Robbins, 1,110; Willie D. Pierce, 983; Bruce P. Wheeler, 931; Zeno Crittenden, 610.

Five amendments to the City Pension plan were approved by majorities of about three to one.

East Detroit

Councilman Harry W. McMillan was elected mayor of East Detroit to succeed Mayor Richard Maxwell, who was not a candidate for re-election.

McMillan defeated William H. Ryan, another councilman, 1,099 to 631.

In the race for two Council posts, the vote was: Allen D. Aschenbach, 1,078; Betty Hays, 720; Clement A. Rock, 640; A. H. Neville, 602. None is a present Council member.

Charles W. Yost defeated Frederick W. Renard for constable, 725 to 642.

Hazel Park

The two incumbent councilmen seeking re-election in Hazel Park were easy victors.

John M. Gray received 804 votes, Benjamin L. Walton 800, Paul Edward Worley 461 and Warren Sturr 331.

Constable Thomas Hegge led Homer R. Pugh, 477 to 292, with one of the city's five precincts unreported.

Pleasant Ridge

Pleasant Ridge returned two incumbent city commissioners to office in a three-man race. The vote was: Edward H. Stanton 289, Harry K. Munroe 253, Ned W. Randau 147.

Dearborn

Dearborn voters registered decisive disapproval of proposals to raise the pay of several City officials $1,500 a year.

A proposed increase for Council members was turned down, 3,027 to 755; a boost in pay for the mayor, City clerk and treasurer was rejected 3,070 to 715, and raises for the municipal judges were defeated, 3,000 to 900.

The sentiment against boosting the City officials' pay carried two strictly routine charter amendments to defeat. One providing immediate effect for ordinances

Turn to Page 2, Column 1

'Pasture' Is Urged for Iowa House

DES MOINES, Ia.—(UP)—Rep. John A. Walker (R.) suggested that the Iowa House be "retired to pasture" Nov. 1, when the House membership reaches an average age of 55.

If the resolution were adopted, the representatives would be retired at half pay, $500 per biennium.

Incumbent Judges Win; State Goes Republican

Late Tabulations

City Returns

RECORDER AND JUDGE OF THE RECORDER'S COURT
(800 out of 1,211 Precincts)

John J. Maher	67,898
Samuel W. Barr	14,996

JUDGES OF THE RECORDER'S COURT
(9 to be elected)

George Murphy	47,069
John P. Scallen	46,804
W. McKay Skillman	46,116
Joseph A. Gillis	45,933
Paul E. Krause	[illegible]
Christopher E. Stein	45,336
O. Z. Ide	44,215
Arthur F. Gordon	42,870
Gerald W. Groat	38,864
Frank G. Schemanske	34,935
Gerald K. O'Brien	33,334
Chas. R. A. Smith	24,965
Jacob L. Keidan	21,548
Edward P. Marschner	19,637
Raymond J. Lynch	17,492
Michael D. McNamara	16,403
Francis J. Mahon	13,593
Bert Robb	11,893

JUDGES OF THE RECORDER'S COURT—TRAFFIC AND ORDINANCE DIVISION
(2 to be elected)

John D. Watts	51,733
George T. Murphy	49,560
Mary V. Beck	24,165
James R. Walsh	22,048

JUDGES OF THE COMMON PLEAS COURT
(Full Term)
(800 Out of 1,211 Precincts)
(4 to be elected)

Thomas A. Kenney	39,692
L. Eugene Sharp	38,512
Harry J. Dingeman, Jr.	31,545
Andrew C. Baird	29,223
George T. Cartwright	29,043
Arthur W. Sempliner	28,514
E. N. Karay	28,087
Eduard Werner	26,995

JUDGES OF THE COMMON PLEAS COURT
(To Fill Vacancies)
(2 to be elected)

Harry J. Dingeman, Jr.	33,072
George T. Cartwright	31,662
Andrew C. Baird	30,145
E. N. Karay	29,690

MEMBERS OF THE BOARD OF EDUCATION
(2 to be elected)

Laura F. Osborn	50,978
Robert G. Foster	49,684
Michael J. O'Brien	44,474
Clark D. Brooks	43,191

CHARTER AMENDMENTS
(Salaries of Councilmen)

NO	67,785
YES	21,219

(General Retirement System)

NO	50,198
YES	38,151

MEMBER OF THE STATE BOARD OF EDUCATION

Victor Targonski (D)	56,630
Louisa I. Durham (R)	88,705

MEMBERS OF THE STATE BOARD OF AGRICULTURE

Clark L. Brody (R)	85,446
Ellsworth B. Moore (R)	64,463
George D. Stevens (D)	60,301
William S. Lamoreaux (D)	56,482

County Returns

CIRCUIT COURT JUDGE
(800 out of 1,486 Precincts)
(18 to be elected)

Thomas F. Maher	52,278
Ella M. Neuenfelt	46,406
John V. Brennan	46,018
Ira W. Jayne	44,726
James E. Chenot	44,689
Chester P. O'Hara	44,239
Joseph A. Moynihan	43,468
Vincent M. Brennan	42,442
George B. Murphy	42,298
Robert M. Toms	[illegible]
Arthur Webster	39,758
Thomas J. Murphy	39,529
Adolph F. Marshner	39,398
Guy A. Miller	39,215
Clyde I. Webster	39,138
Theodore J. Richter	38,535
Frank Fitzgerald	34,448
Frank B. Ferguson	32,362
William E. Dowling	30,159
Ned H. Smith	28,460
George D. O'Brien	28,279
Henry S. Sweeny	[illegible]
Gerald F. Fitzgerald	22,402
William Friedman	21,356
S. B. Keidan	17,073
George Bashara	19,092
V. E. Sacre	[illegible]
Arthur Cyrowski	15,976
Henry G. Nicol	15,013
James Montante	14,027
Samuel W. Leib	13,912
Charles E. Merrill	13,014
Harrison T. Watson	11,697
William Brashear	10,873
George P. Coash	10,336
Francis M. Trexler	10,107

COUNTY AUDITOR
(800 out of 1,486 Precincts)

Jacob P. Sumeracki (D)	58,231
John A. Kronk (R)	41,186

State Returns

JUSTICE OF SUPREME COURT
(Full Term)
(1,246 out of 3,968 Precincts)

Leland W. Carr	96,934
Henry M. Butzel	76,789
Edward T. Kane	46,268
Patrick S. Nertney	27,561

JUSTICE OF SUPREME COURT
(Term Ending Dec. 31, 1953)

John R. Dethmers	[illegible]
Maurice E. Tripp	35,639

PROPOSAL NO. ONE

YES	70,766
NO	63,023

PROPOSAL NO. TWO

NO	63,164
YES	58,909

REGENTS OF THE UNIVERSITY

J. Joseph Herbert (R)	84,351
Kenneth M. Stevens (R)	83,775
George D. Schermerhorn (D)	59,330
John L. Brumm (D)	58,780

SUPERINTENDENT OF PUBLIC INSTRUCTION

Eugene B. Elliott (R)	89,475
George F. Montgomery (D)	60,563

U.S. May Ask Full Fine on Miners

New York Times Service

WASHINGTON—Government attorneys, it was learned, will ask Federal Judge T. Alan Goldsborough Thursday to restore the contempt fine against the United Mine Workers (AFL) to the full amount of $3,500,000 set by him last December.

They will ask this action as a result of the current mine "safety" work stoppage.

* * *

THE GOVERNMENT will charge that UMW Chief John L. Lewis and the union have displayed bad faith and trickery in tying up the mines in this manner after the Supreme Court upheld the lower court's injunction barring a strike against the Government.

The high court ruled that if Lewis obeyed the no-strike edict, $2,800,000 of the fine would be returned to the union.

Lewis withdrew his strike notice after the miners had been out three weeks, but the current unofficial stoppage has curtailed operations again.

6 Drown in Gale

PARIS—(UP)—Six persons drowned when a hurricane swamped a fishing boat off France's western coast.

City Charter Amendments Are Beaten

Sumeracki Defeats Kronk for Auditor

BY HUB M. GEORGE
Free Press Staff Writer

Michigan electors swept back into office three justices of the State Supreme Court, named Republicans for all State offices and rejected three of the four special ballot proposals.

Disturbed communications as a result of the telephone strike caused returns to trickle in.

Voting was the lightest in a decade, reflecting complications of floods and washouts as well as public apathy.

* * *

ALL INCUMBENT Circuit Judges appeared to have been re-elected with Frank FitzGerald, court commissioner, chosen for the place left vacant when Judge Sherman D. Callender decided not to seek re-election.

Recorder's Judge John J. Maher and nine associates on that bench also were re-elected. The runners-up were Gerald K. O'Brien, former prosecutor, and Frank G. Shemanske, former assistant prosecutor.

Traffic Judges George T Murphy and John D. Watts, withstood the challenge of Mary V. Beck and James R. Walsh.

* * *

THE DAY'S biggest upsets were the probable defeat of Common Pleas Judges George T. Cartwright and Emanuel N. Karey, both appointees of former Gov. Kelly.

Judges Thomas A. Kenney, also a Kelly appointee and L. Eugene Sharpe were re-elected.

The two additional places on the bench appeared won by Harry J. Dingeman, Jr., son of the former Circuit Judge, and Andrew C. Baird, former sheriff.

The voters likewise retired Dr. Clark D. Brooks, former president of the Detroit Board of Education, but gave Mrs. Laura Osborn, a board veteran, a vote of confidence. Her associate will be Robert G. Foster, at present a teacher.

* * *

CITY CHARTER amendments to boost councilmen's pay from $5,000 to $7,500 a year and to liberalize the Retirement System were defeated.

So was the state constitutional amendment to permit corporations to hold income property for 30 instead of 10 years. The amendment to skip judicial primaries where there are no contests was approved.

Returns expressed public confidence in the conduct of recent grand juries.

* * *

JUSTICE Leland W. Carr, who was associated with Gov. Sigler in the Ingham County grand jury, led six aspirants for the Supreme Court with a substantial margin.

Judge George B. Murphy, labor-rackets grand juror, was well up among the Circuit Court candidates.

Republican and Democratic candidates for State office ran neck and neck in Wayne County, but County Auditor Jacob P. Sumeracki, Democrat, outdistanced his rival, John A. Kronk, Republican, in the only County partisan contest.

Strike Foiled

LISBON—(AP)—The Portuguese Government, moving to halt spreading strikes in Lisbon's waterfront and industrial areas, ordered troops to replace dock workers.

Newspapers mourned the great industrialist's passing.

In 1943, Henry and Clara's only son, Edsel Ford, who was an able and enthusiastic supporter of the museum and the arts in general, died of stomach cancer at the age of forty-nine. Two years later, Henry Ford suffered a severe stroke. Eighty-three-year-old Henry Ford died on April 7, 1947, at Fair Lane, his Dearborn home, with his wife Clara by his side. To allow the public to pay their respects, Ford lay in state at the Edison Institute, his body resting in the lobby of Lovett Hall. He was buried in a Ford family cemetery on the grounds of St. Martha's Episcopal Church on Joy Road in Detroit, near his mother and father.

The passing of the Edison Institute's founder begged the question "what next?" for the institution. Henry Ford's vision had been the driving force behind his creation. Who would drive that vision now?

A student lowered the flag at Henry Ford's Scotch Settlement School to half-staff upon hearing of his death.

"[Mr. Ford] expected someday to leave. Just how he thought it was going to be carried on, I don't know."

– Roy Schumann, Edison Institute Employee, *Reminiscences*

FACT:
Henry Ford passed away at Fair Lane when the electricity went out because of a storm. He was born in a room illuminated by candles and oil lamps, and died that way, too.

CHAPTER 2

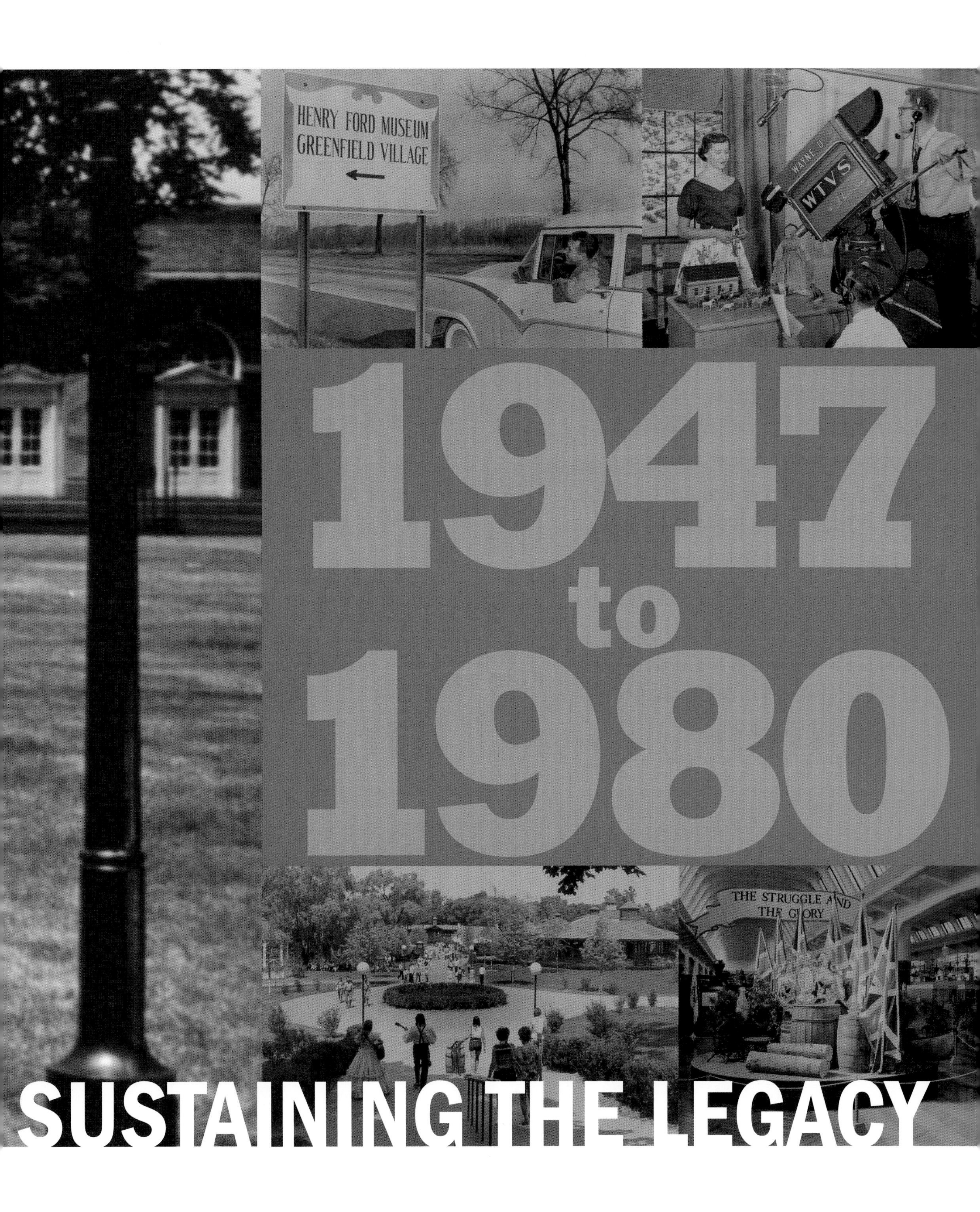

1947 to 1980

SUSTAINING THE LEGACY

a search for New Leadership and Vision

"Since its inception, the Institute has been in . . . its acquisition period. From now on it . . . should enter its interpretive period. But what should be interpreted? What job do you want to do? What are you?"

– Allyston Boyer, Report to A. K. Mills, 1951

Henry Ford had created The Edison Institute according to his own personal vision.

For eighteen years, Henry Ford's energy had been the animating force behind The Edison Institute.

He never implemented much of a formal management system—he ran the show. Ford's death left the institution adrift—awash in a wealth of historical collections and challenged by a lack of direction and financial stability. Ford left no money to The Edison Institute; the Ford Foundation was his beneficiary.

The break from Henry Ford's autocratic rule created inevitable struggles for control. Ford's subordinates had possessed varying degrees of influence over the museum and village but never official authority. Although some had built small empires, they always had to depend on Ford's support when a dispute arose—staying in Henry Ford's good graces always proved vital to their survival. An official chain of command had never emerged.

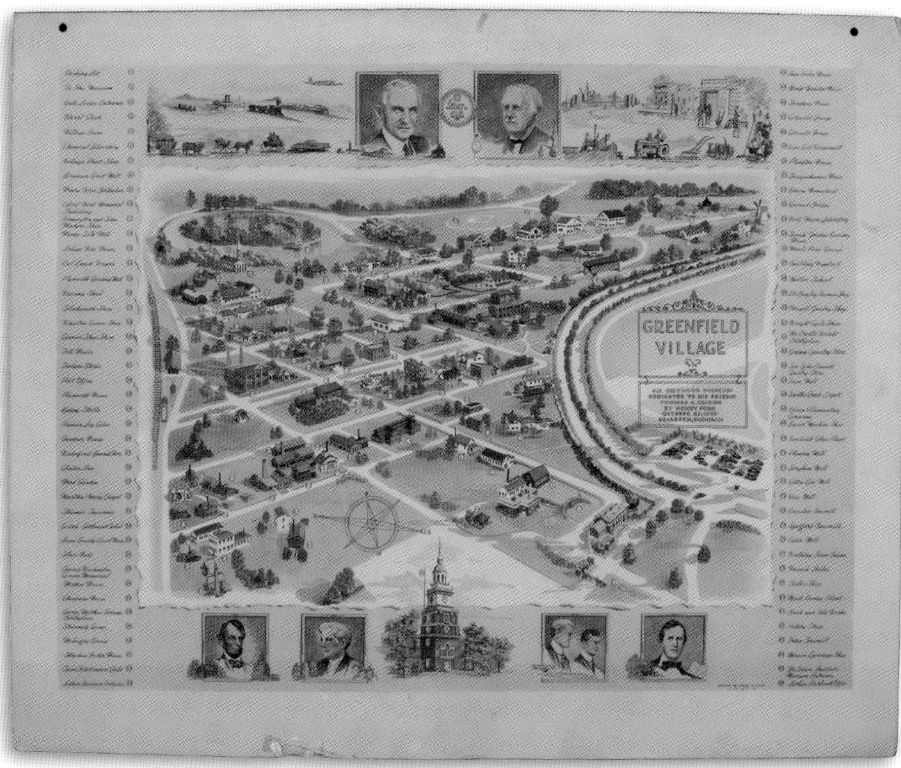

Map of Greenfield Village, 1951.

For the first few years after Ford's death, the skeletal staff maintained the status quo—fulfilling their duties with no direction and simply doing what they thought Mr. Ford would have wanted. Ford's wife, Clara, who took over for her husband, met weekly with the museum and village staff and encouraged them to "do as Mr. Ford did." Any change that ran contrary to Ford's vision disturbed her.

The museum and village were being operated as two separate organizations, neither running very efficiently or effectively.

In 1949, the Board of Trustees appointed Hayward S. Ablewhite director of the museum, and with his appointment came the institution's first organizational chart that clearly defined job duties and created and streamlined departments. The death of Clara Ford in 1950 signaled the end of an era. Her last gesture of support for her husband's "hobby" was to leave The Edison Institute a generous $4 million bequest.

(Opposite) A postcard of the car display, early 1950s.

This gift, however, did not diminish the institute's need for a sustainable business plan, as it now had no stable financial base. For years, expenses

Mrs. Ford's interest was in preserving her husband's hobby. She bridled at any changes to the status quo.

for the museum and village had vastly exceeded revenue. The shortfall had been always made up by Henry Ford and, after his death, by the Ford Foundation. In the early 1950s, museum leadership faced the challenge of making the institution increasingly self-supporting.

The Ford family stepped away from active daily management of the institution and began a strong tradition of lay leadership. In the early 1950s, all three of Henry Ford's grandsons served on the Board of Trustees—Henry Ford II, the oldest of the grandsons, joined the board in 1943; Benson Ford was board president from 1947 to 1951; his younger brother, William Clay Ford, took over in 1951 and held the position of president, then chairman of the board for thirty-eight years. In 1989 he became chairman emeritus.

In January 1951, the board appointed A. K. Mills, director of Ford Motor Company's Fiftieth Anniversary Plans Office and a close friend of Henry Ford II, to the new post of executive director with responsibility—on paper and in practice—for both Greenfield Village and the Edison Institute Museum. Mills took his new position seriously. In order to gain a wider perspective about the museum field, in 1953, Mills visited thirty indoor and outdoor museums in Europe to learn what similar institutions were doing.

Mills implemented established business practices and hired professional staff members, including Donald Shelley, who served as curator of fine arts. When Mills died suddenly in 1954, Donald Shelley replaced him as executive director, remaining at the helm for the next twenty-two years.

William Clay Ford is shown here in 1953 on the Ford test track behind the wheel of his grandfather's famous racecar, the 999. The museum clock tower can be seen in the distance.

(Left) In 1952, an eight-foot-high serpentine brick wall was built by the Ford Motor Company to separate the Ford Test Track from Village Road. It signified the growing autonomy of village and museum operations from the company.

(Below) The museum made a monthly request to the Ford Foundation to make up its deficit. This request for $100,000 is for the month of February 1949.

Form 175

DEPARTMENTAL COMMUNICATION

Date 1-27 19 49

To Mr. B. J. Craig Dept. Ford Foundation

This is to remind you that The Edison Institute will require $100,000.00 for the month of February, 1949. This is part of the $650,000.00 requested in our letter to the Ford Foundation dated December 23, 1948.

THE EDISON INSTITUTE

Frank Caddy

FC RC

Dept.

Signed

"It seems to me that the first step which should be taken is to define both the Museum and Greenfield Village. Without a clear definition of what they are and what they are trying to accomplish, they cannot grow intelligently, they cannot do a satisfactory, educational job nor can they assume their rightful place in the field of great American museums."

– Allston Boyer, Assistant to the President, Colonial Williamsburg, April 1951

managing the Collections

"The files were in a deplorable condition. If you wanted to find out about something, it was just hit-or-miss . . . Everything was filed alphabetically in just a hodgepodge."

– Hayward Ablewhite, Museum Director, *Reminiscences*

Ford's death challenged the institution to manage a collection–that had grown to massive proportions–with no adequate storage solutions and no formal cataloging system.

Staff quietly stored artifacts in museum attics and basement utility tunnels, and in the 1950s, employees began the colossal task of organizing files, inventorying the artifacts, and cataloging the individual objects in the collection.

With no real in-depth research on the artifacts and historic structures, it was no surprise that the information visitors heard on their tours was often incomplete or inaccurate. Exhibits offered little in the way of explanatory labels, and with the lack of trained guides, security guards and other employees would try to fill the void with their own versions of history.

Henry Ford, himself, contributed to the confusion. For example, when Ford acquired the Foster home in the mid-1930s, he was told by the composer's daughter that the Pennsylvania home was indeed Foster's birthplace. Ford accepted the daughter's recollection as fact. However, thorough research conducted in 1953 confirmed that Foster's actual birthplace had been torn down in 1865.

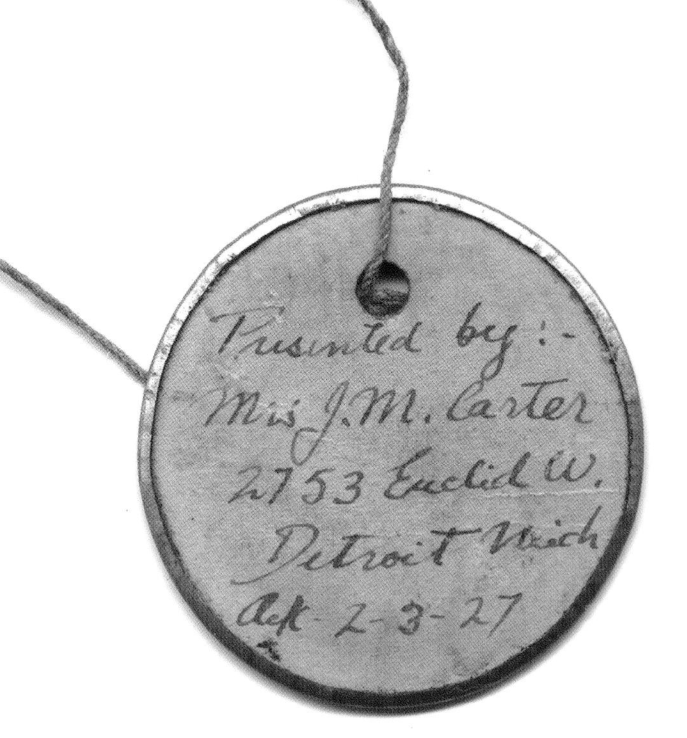

One of the tags used to identify objects.

(Opposite) As the collection grew, objects that could not be squeezed into the already overcrowded museum displays were squirreled away. Chairs, for example, were stacked in the back of the museum.

A variety of tags were used to identify objects.

Artifacts such as this hand milking machine were not recognizable to a younger generation.

Detroit Free Press

Friday, January 30, 1953 THE SECOND FRONT PAGE

This is the house which Henry Ford restored

Stephen Foster Home In Museum Wrong One

BY CLINT WILKINSON
Free Press Staff Writer

A long-standing argument was ended Thursday—once and for all.

The house in Greenfield Village which purports to be the birthplace of Stephen C. Foster is an imposter.

The announcement signaled the victorious end of an 18-year fight by a niece of the composer, Mrs. A. C. Morneweck, a Detroiter of 25 years' standing who lives at 5056 Underwood.

The Greenfield Village house and the actual birthplace of Foster stood some 200 yards apart, a report from trustees of the Henry Ford Museum established. The report was written by Dr. Milo M. Quaife, an outstanding Detroit historian.

* * *

THE ACTUAL Foster birthplace was torn down in 1865 and replaced by a brick building which is now one wing of a funeral home in Pittsburgh. The funeral home stands on part of the original foundation of the Foster homestead.

A shabby old frame house, which once lay in Lawrenceville, Pa., was the Foster birthplace, an agent of the late Henry Ford decided.

Piece by piece, it was sent to Detroit. The Ford researchers restored the aged building to what they believed was its original appearance.

With fanfare, the house was proclaimed to be the Foster birthplace and dedicated in Greenfield Village on July 4, 1935, at impressive ceremonies.

* * *

MRS. MORNEWECK, daughter of the composer's elder brother, Morrison, was not convinced.

She had the family property records, cached in boxes in the attic. She inspected them. They showed that the reconstructed house was not the one where Foster was born.

Almost no one was convinced for some time, except John Tasker Howard, Foster's biographer.

"I went to Mr. Ford," Mrs. Morneweck said. "He told me that he had been told it was the right house and said, 'That's good enough for me.' "

She added: "We've been certain he was wrong all along."

* * *

MRS. MORNEWECK was not among the relatives who gathered for the dedication ceremonies—although she was invited.

The composer's own daughter had been slated to attend. The daughter, then 84, was old and infirm. She insisted that the Greenfield Village house was her father's birthplace.

The Greenfield Village home—like all those in Lawrenceville of that day—was located on land owned by Foster's father. He lost the heavily mortgaged land in May, 1826.

Today it would be worth a fortune.

Its authenticity disproved, the remodeled house still will stand as a memorial to the composer who gave the world such songs as "Old Black Joe" and "Old Folks at Home."

A newspaper article reported on the misidentification of the Stephen Foster Home.

honoring the Founder

"I have had the opportunity to see him at work as a country-boy mechanic and later as a world figure. Here in the Henry Ford Room are gathered both objects and papers that mark the milestones on his road to success."

– Margaret Ford Ruddiman, Henry Ford's sister, *Henry Ford: A Personal History*, 1953

In 1952, as a tribute to its founder, The Edison Institute, incorporated by Henry Ford in 1929, was renamed Henry Ford Museum and Greenfield Village.

Brochures, maps, and guidebooks were quickly produced with the new name and a new logo—an image that featured the clock tower and Henry Ford, driving his first automobile, the Quadricycle.

The next year, 1953, marked the fiftieth anniversary of Ford Motor Company and the ninetieth anniversary of Henry Ford's birth, and further provided opportunities for the organization to honor Ford.

Two significant experiences emerged that year—the Dearborn farmhouse in which Henry Ford had been born, opened to the public for the first time (though it had been moved to the village in 1944, it remained closed), and a new exhibit, *Henry Ford: A Personal History*, opened in Henry Ford Museum.

The exhibit, the first major addition to the museum since Ford's death, was a collaborative effort between the organization and the recently established Ford Motor Company Archives. The display featured photographs, letters, account books, and receipts from the Ford Archives, along with Ford-related artifacts from the museum's collection and offered an intriguing look at Henry Ford's life. A full-scale recreation of Henry Ford's office—complete with original oak paneling and office furniture—as it appeared in January 1914, when Ford made his famous announcement offering an unheard wage of five dollars a day to the workers on the Ford assembly line, was the exhibit's centerpiece.

A Henry Ford Museum brochure from the early 1950s with the new logo incorporating the museum clock tower and Henry Ford driving the Quadricycle, his first car.

(Opposite) Visitors enter Henry Ford Birthplace in Greenfield Village.

(Above) A major feature of *Henry Ford: A Personal History* was the recreation of Henry Ford's 1914 office.

Entrance to the exhibit *Henry Ford: A Personal History.*

The Edison Institute
Dearborn, Michigan

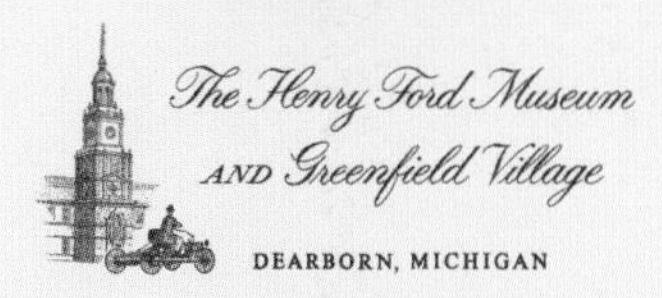

THE EDISON INSTITUTE
Henry Ford Museum
& Greenfield Village

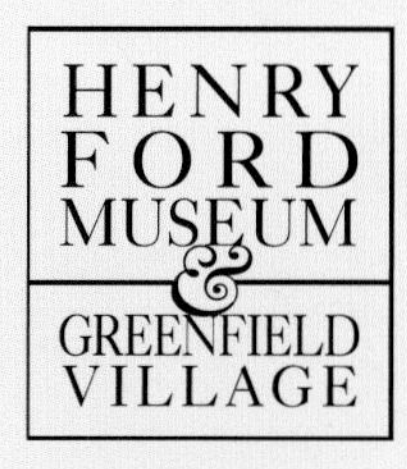

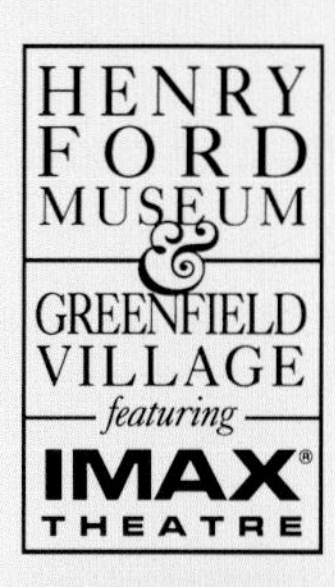

America's Greatest History Attraction

What's In a Name?

The Henry Ford's name has always been a source of confusion. Here is a brief chronology:

1929: Incorporated as The Edison Institute

1929–1951: Identified as The Edison Institute Museum and Village

1952: In memory of the founder, the museum is named Henry Ford Museum.

1973: Henry Ford Museum and Greenfield Village becomes the institution's name.

1973–1980: The name order is reversed to Greenfield Village and Henry Ford Museum.

1981–1985: The order reverts to Henry Ford Museum & Greenfield Village, but with an ampersand this time. An attempt to incorporate the original name—The Edison Institute—is unsuccessful.

1986–1999: The public use of The Edison Institute is dropped although it remains the legal name. It's now just Henry Ford Museum & Greenfield Village.

1999–2002: The opening of the IMAX Theatre lengthens the name to Henry Ford Museum & Greenfield Village featuring IMAX Theatre.

2003–: The Henry Ford becomes the official destination name, serving as the umbrella for the growing list of attractions including Henry Ford Museum, Greenfield Village, Ford Rouge Factory Tour, IMAX Theatre, and Benson Ford Research Center.

a national Institution

"All our efforts were directed to the task of securing broad recognition of Henry Ford Museum and Greenfield Village as 'the' outstanding Museum of American History devoted to educational work."

Annual Report, 1955-56

During the 1950s, the public—especially the vast traveling public—became the focus of the institution's attention.

For the first time, the museum and village began to actively market itself to local, regional, and national audiences.

A. K. Mills, the museum and village's executive director in the early 1950s, came from a public relations background and was responsible for the organization's first set of advertising billboards and directional signs placed along Michigan highways. Further assistance for the motoring public came in the form of specially printed maps distributed to local gas stations, motels, and restaurants.

Articles in widely read magazines, such as *National Geographic* and *Antiques*, provided valuable national exposure, while articles in travel industry publications and displays at travel shows encouraged visits from tourists. A series of licensing agreements in the 1950s and 1960s to create reproduction home furnishings further increased the institution's name recognition. Woodbury Pewterers, Century Furniture, and Fostoria Glass, among others, manufactured items, such as pewter, furniture, and glassware, based on specially selected items from the collection.

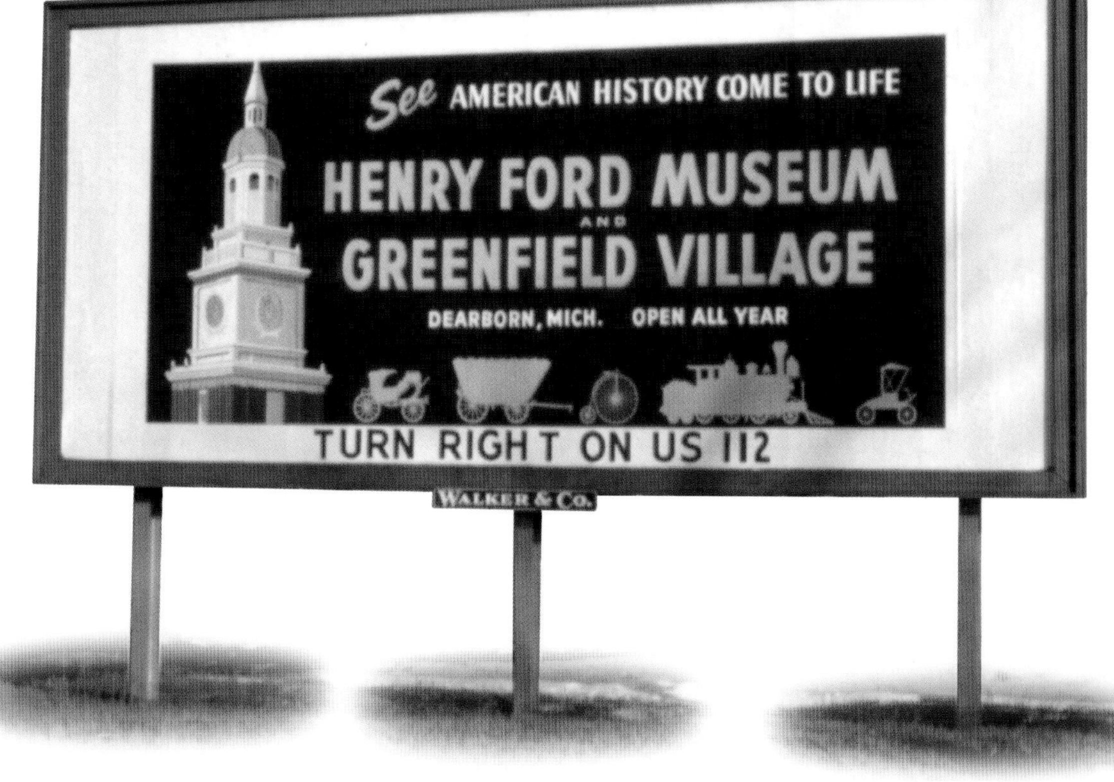

(Above and opposite) Billboards and signs to the museum and village began to appear on Michigan highways in the 1950s.

Traveling exhibits, developed by the institution in the 1950s, offered the museum a chance to promote itself beyond the local area, increase awareness, and, hopefully, increase visitation. A series of "railroad car" exhibits, filled with the collections of Henry Ford Museum and showcasing progress in American industry, education, and domestic life, toured the country for several years and were seen by millions of people across America.

Decorating ideas from historic Greenfield Village

By EVAN FRANCES
FURNISHINGS EDITOR

IN Dearborn, Michigan, are the Henry Ford Museum and Greenfield Village, founded in the late 1920s to trace, display, preserve, and venerate three centuries of America's arts and skills. Here, in transplanted historic houses (among them, Stephen Foster's, Luther Burbank's, and Noah Webster's), are treasured antiques. Beyond seeing and exulting in our abundant past, your visit can enrich your present and future living, for you can adapt decorative ideas from the houses and see true reproductions of many of their antiques — available today, thanks to the museum's painstaking reproduction program. Join us on a journey to a glorious past, vicariously now, through these eight pages of FAMILY CIRCLE. Then go, if you can, and revel at firsthand.

Interior design for Plymouth House by Thomas A. McEvoy, A.I.D., and James Cantler
All photos by Bill Hedrich — Hedrich-Blessing

Above and left are photos of the dining room in Plymouth House, an 1830 Greenfield Village home, typical of the modest kind of its time. We asked that it be furnished with some of the impeccable reproductions the museum has authorized selected manufacturers to produce today and make available to you at moderate prices through leading stores across the country. Outstanding is the pine hunt board, the original of which is vintage 1800. It was usually kept in the back of the house and carried outside to be used for venison carving. The dining table is adapted from 18th-century designs into a rectangular extension table. The originals of the Queen Anne chairs, from New Hampshire, date from 1720-40. The original of the small five-sided table and of the hooked rug are shown on page 54 (Burbank house); of the barrel chair, on page 56 (Foster house). Fabrics, lighting, candles, glassware, pewter, flatware, bottles are copies

ON THE COVER
Living room of Plymouth House—shown in color on the cover and in other views on the next two pages. At the right of the Stephen Foster barrel chair is a candlestand, reproduced from an 18th-century Pennsylvania original, unique in having two square tiers. Its simple heavy feet are typical of the practicality of the country cabinetmaker's art. Our "coffee table" is a true copy of an 1800 tilt-top candlestand

50 FAMILY CIRCLE OCTOBER 1965

MORE

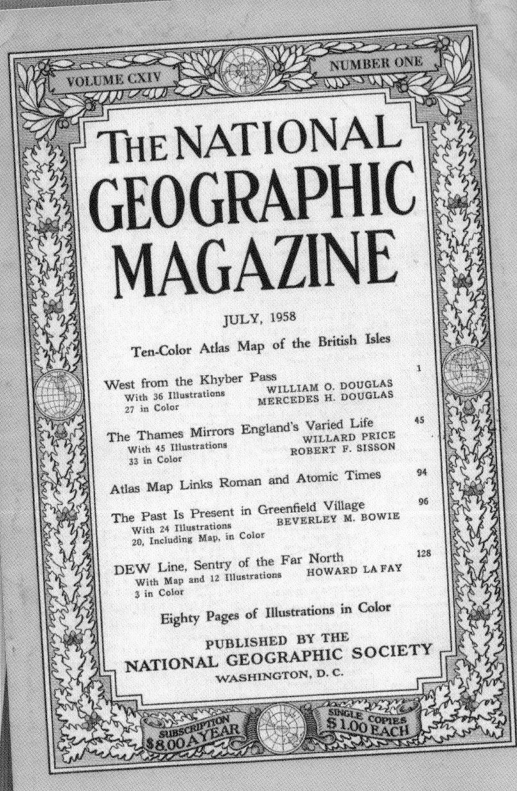

VOLUME CXIV NUMBER ONE

THE NATIONAL GEOGRAPHIC MAGAZINE

JULY, 1958

Ten-Color Atlas Map of the British Isles

West from the Khyber Pass With 36 Illustrations 27 in Color	WILLIAM O. DOUGLAS MERCEDES H. DOUGLAS	1
The Thames Mirrors England's Varied Life With 45 Illustrations 33 in Color	WILLARD PRICE ROBERT F. SISSON	45
Atlas Map Links Roman and Atomic Times		94
The Past Is Present in Greenfield Village With 24 Illustrations 20, Including Map, in Color	BEVERLEY M. BOWIE	96
DEW Line, Sentry of the Far North With Map and 12 Illustrations 3 in Color	HOWARD LA FAY	128

Eighty Pages of Illustrations in Color

PUBLISHED BY THE NATIONAL GEOGRAPHIC SOCIETY
WASHINGTON, D. C.

SUBSCRIPTION $8.00 A YEAR   SINGLE COPIES $1.00 EACH

(Above left) An article in *Family Circle* magazine, October 1965, featured the museum's reproduction program. The program continued to the early 1980s.

(Above right) The museum successfully courted the publicity of nationally distributed magazines like *National Geographic* and *Antiques*.

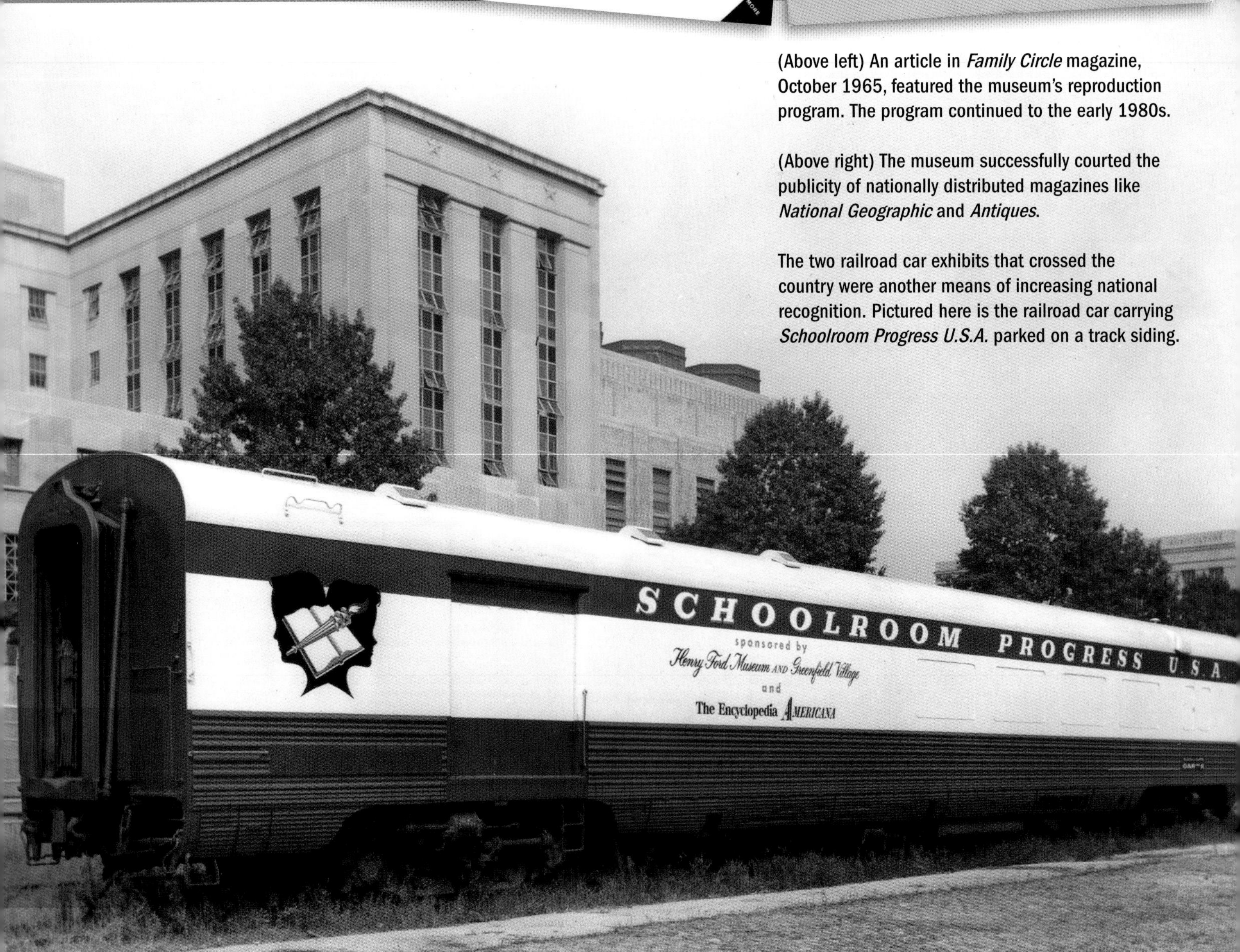

The two railroad car exhibits that crossed the country were another means of increasing national recognition. Pictured here is the railroad car carrying *Schoolroom Progress U.S.A.* parked on a track siding.

The new medium of television proved especially powerful in reaching new audiences. On October 25, 1955, NBC-TV aired three live programs from Greenfield Village—the *Today* show broadcast early morning chapel services, while later that morning, Arlene Francis's *Home* show offered a look at a "typical" day in a mid-nineteenth-century village and the *Howdy Doody Show*, featuring the Greenfield Village schoolchildren, broadcast that afternoon from Scotch Settlement School.

FACT:
In 1953, the museum acquired the nearby Dearborn Inn as a gift from the Ford Motor Company—adding a fifty-four-room addition in 1960 to accommodate the increasing numbers of travelers. The museum owned the inn for thirty-one years before selling it back to Ford Motor Company in 1984.

Henry Ford Museum's attendance steadily climbed each year. The number of visitors doubled over the decade, from five hundred thousand in 1950 to one million by 1960. The village and museum had become a national attraction.

Greenfield Village schoolchildren surrounded the cast of the *Howdy Doody Show* during the live telecast from Greenfield Village in 1955.

new
Programs and Audiences

"You know, I wish Mr. Ford had been here today. He would have gotten a kick out of all those old cars and the kids gawking at them, and the village really coming to life."

–Ralph Shackleton, employee commenting on Old Car Festival, *National Geographic*, 1958

During the 1950s and the 1960s, the museum prepared to engage a new generation of visitors.

Fresh paint, improved exhibits, special events, and enhanced amenities began to transform the museum into an increasingly attractive destination for the visiting public.

In Henry Ford Museum, curators reduced the number of objects on display in the main exhibit hall, arranged the artifacts in a more orderly fashion, and provided explanatory labels. The transportation collections were rearranged, presenting the trains, automobiles, and bicycles in chronological order for the first time. This helped visitors see more clearly how technology and design had evolved over time. Similarly, the decorative arts galleries grouped furniture, ceramics, glassware, and silver to show the evolution of American taste.

Furniture, ceramics, and silver were displayed in the transformed decorative arts galleries in the front corridor of the museum.

(Opposite) Early automobiles filled the village green during Old Car Festival.

A roster of changing exhibits—as many as six a year—offered new ways of looking at the collections.

To broaden audience appeal, Henry Ford Museum developed a series of programs to appeal to special interests—lecture series, movie festivals, live theater, and special events. In the 1960s and 1970s, the annual Midwest Antiques Forum sponsored lectures on antique furniture and decorative arts, while the Famous Early Movie Festival showed classic silent and sound comedies, westerns, and adventure films in the museum's theater (now Anderson Theater). In 1964, the American Drama Festival debuted with its presentation of early American plays. By the end of the 1970s, the year-round theater season alternated traditional nineteenth-century plays with American classics from the first half of the twentieth century, as well as children's plays presented at the holiday season, such as *Rumplestiltskin* and *Peter Pan*. In the summer of 1971, the theater company began presenting live performances in Greenfield Village, including medicine shows, musical entertainment, and vignettes from the lives of famous Americans.

With the increase in attendance, the staff began to build on the experiences in Greenfield Village. The Suwanee steamboat operated

A Luncheon Suggestion

For a pleasant mid-day break in your Greenfield Village visit, plan to enjoy luncheon cafeteria style, in the historic Clinton Inn on the Village Green. We'll be looking forward to seeing you.

Bill of Fare

subject to change

Item	Price
Juices	.15
Greenfield Village Baked Ham Sandwich Plate	.65
Susqehanna Salad Plate	.50
Waterford Tuna Salad Sandwich Plate	.50
Plymouth Egg Salad Sandwich Plate	.50
Jordan Boarding House Plate	.60
Currier Cold Plate	.90
Clinton Inn Bean Soup and Crackers	.30
Martha-Mary Salad Bowl	.25
Loranger Cherry Wholewheat Muffin with Butter	.10
Hard Roll with Butter	.10
Iced Coffee and Tea	.10
Hot Coffee and Tea	.10
Milk (White or Chocolate)	.10
Ann Arbor Cherry Pie	.20
Sarah Jordan Apple Pie	.20
Ice Cream—(Chocolate, Vanilla and Strawberry)	.15

Clinton Inn

GREENFIELD VILLAGE, DEARBORN, MICHIGAN

(Top) Visitors to Greenfield Village's General Store (now J. R. Jones General Store) saw goods available to nineteenth-century shoppers, and enjoyed a taste of old-fashioned candy, 1965.

(Above right) Famous Early Movie Festival brochure, 1962.

(Above left) A Clinton Inn (now Eagle Tavern) menu from about 1952.

regularly, and Model T rides were added in the late 1950s. Buildings in the refurbished industrial area, like the Tripp sawmill, opened to the public for the first time since the early 1930s, and the interiors of the historic homes, filled with must-see period furnishings from the museum's collections, became a bigger part of the daily program.

Craft demonstrations added another layer of activity for patrons. Visitors loved to watch as craftspeople forged iron tools, blew glass, or dipped candles. The village did a brisk business selling such souvenirs as hand-woven bookmarks, nail rings, hand-dipped candles, or flour that had been ground at the Loranger gristmill.

In 1951, the village launched two special events, Country Fair of Yesteryear and Old Car Festival. Country Fair of Yesteryear, which offered a mixture of activities such as a barbershop quartet, dancing on the green, antique carriages and automobiles, a minstrel show, crafts,

(Above) Landscaping also received attention during the mid-1950s. To emphasize its regional origins in tidewater Maryland, Susquehanna House acquired a seventeenth-century-style formal garden, complete with oyster shell paths.

1. Since first introduced in 1958, the Model T ride has remained a favorite with visitors.

2. The first addition to the village after Henry Ford's death was the 1854 Heinz House from Sharpsburg, Pennsylvania. In 1904, the house became a visitor center for the Heinz Company factory until it came to Greenfield Village in 1953.

3. In 1951, the Suwanee steamboat served as a backdrop for Country Fair of Yesteryear's minstrel show.

4. When it opened to the public in 1958, Luther Burbank's Massachusetts birthplace featured folk art decorations and country painted furniture.

5. In the 1960s and 1970s, at Muzzle Loaders Festival, hundreds of Civil War reenactors competed at target shooting using reproduction firearms.

(Below) Dipping candles for visitors to purchase.

In the Loranger gristmill, grain was ground into flour that could be purchased by visitors.

(Below) Visitors enjoyed leisurely carriage rides through the village.

and a firefighting demonstration, ended in the early 1980s. Old Car Festival, which includes an enormous display of antique vehicles, is still hosted by Greenfield Village and is currently the longest-running antique car gathering in the world.

Over the years, additional themed events debuted. The Greenfield Village Turkey Shoot, soon renamed Muzzle Loaders Festival, a Civil War–era program featuring shooting competitions with live ammunition, had a lengthy run after its introduction in 1955. The event was discontinued in the early 1980s owing to safety concerns.

In the 1950s, in addition to expanding the village's experiences and activities, the decision was made to expand the outdoor museum's inventory, and for the first time since Henry Ford's death, historic buildings were

"The days of lounging in the Village barn are over for our horses. Now that visitors are streaming through, all six teams have been hitched up and are ready to begin another summer of transporting our guests through the wonders of Greenfield Village."

– *Greenfield Villager,* May 1, 1951

(Left) The Doc Bryson Medicine Show was one of the most popular of the summer entertainments in the village, attracting crowds of up to three hundred people.

(Below left) In Greenfield Village, actors brought to life the stories of famous Americans, offering a new way to learn history. This is a depiction of the famous Lincoln-Douglas debates of 1858 that launched Abraham Lincoln into national prominence.

(Below right) This 1964 flyer advertised the first year of the American Drama Festival.

added to Greenfield Village. In 1953, the Heinz Company donated the birthplace of company founder H. J. Heinz, and in 1963, the village received the Michigan office of physician Alonson B. Howard.

As the institution became more aware of the need to increase visitation, it began to invest in improved visitor amenities. The earliest food service for Greenfield Village visitors, the Owl Lunch Wagon, was a basic snack bar, offering simple foods such as hamburgers and hot dogs. In 1951, the Clinton Inn cafeteria (now Eagle Tavern) opened to the public with a themed menu and offerings named for Greenfield Village buildings, such as the "Martha-Mary Salad Bowl." The restaurant also used vegetables from the Greenfield Village gardens and baked pies and cakes with flour ground at the Loranger gristmill. Visitors to Henry Ford Museum had limited eating options until the 1950s, when the Garden Room Cafeteria opened to serve museum visitors.

(Below) Sports Cars in Review, 1957.

new Directions in Education

"We won't forget the kids. It would be difficult in any event; the way they swarm here sometimes makes us think the rest of the United States must look depopulated."

– **Donald Shelley, President**

When Henry Ford died in 1947, he left no instructions regarding the continuing operation of the Edison Institute Schools.

Resources were limited. The high school, in particular, was costly to operate. While it offered a good education, it was not substantially different from other high schools in the area. In contrast, the elementary school curriculum was more closely aligned with Henry Ford's educational vision and intent on providing instruction based on "learning by doing." Eighteen years after it was founded, the Edison Institute High School closed in June 1952, leaving only the elementary grades in operation.

Classes for kindergarten through sixth grade continued in seven village buildings under the name Greenfield Village Schools. Many aspects of Henry Ford's educational vision remained, although educators began to incorporate new methods and instructional materials into their classrooms. Students still tended gardens, explored the historic buildings and artifacts, tried their hand at weaving and pottery, and studied nature. Ultimately, the small number of students did not justify the rising costs of this unique learning experience, and the Greenfield Village Schools closed in 1969.

Students on field trips had been a mainstay for decades, but no special tours or educational materials had ever been created for them. As attention shifted from the school program to the daily visitor, the institution now began to develop special educational programs for students and the general public. A newly created Education Department, established in the 1950s, began to organize tours for visiting school groups, including an overnight program that provided dormitory-style lodging in the Education Building (now Lovett Hall).

The increased emphasis on education led to more information listed on exhibit labels and more properly trained guides for the museum and village. Henry Ford Museum also began producing public television programs for students in classrooms and for families at home. *Window to the Past,* which debuted in 1955 in a public television broadcast, was viewed weekly by elementary students in schools in metropolitan Detroit. Using objects, film clips, and special effects, museum staff made artifacts, and their stories came alive in the classroom.

(Top) *Greenfield Village Schools Handbook, 1964–1965.*

(Above) For almost two decades, student reporters chronicled their school activities in the *Herald*, a monthly student publication.

(Opposite) Fourth grade students in their Town Hall classroom in the 1960s.

(Top) Students plant a garden in this 1967 photograph.

(Right) Marion Corwell films *Window to the Past*, a Detroit-area public television broadcast, in the 1950s.

In the early 1970s, as the pace of activity quickened, museum educators developed a range of themed lesson plans for teachers. The program "A Day in a One-Room School," at Miller School in 1972, was so popular that McGuffey School opened for the same purpose in 1976. Students attending the one-room school program at Miller School dressed in nineteenth-century-style costumes, wrote their lessons on slates, and studied from McGuffey Readers. This hands-on experience was extremely popular with students and their teachers and was offered for several decades.

Courses for adults were popular as well. By the 1970s, adults could choose from a range of classes including chair caning, weaving, rug hooking, and cooking over an open fire.

Although the Greenfield Village Schools had closed, the institution's educational programs now reached tens of thousands of children and adults each year.

Tens of thousands of schoolchildren visited the museum and village each year.

The Automobile teachers' guide from 1972 is an example of material produced by the Education Department to support teachers.

Students attending the one-room school program at Miller School dressed in nineteenth-century-style costumes, and learned with nineteenth-century-style teaching techniques. This hands-on experience has remained extremely popular with students and teachers and is still offered today.

(Below) An open hearth cooking class for adults, 1978.

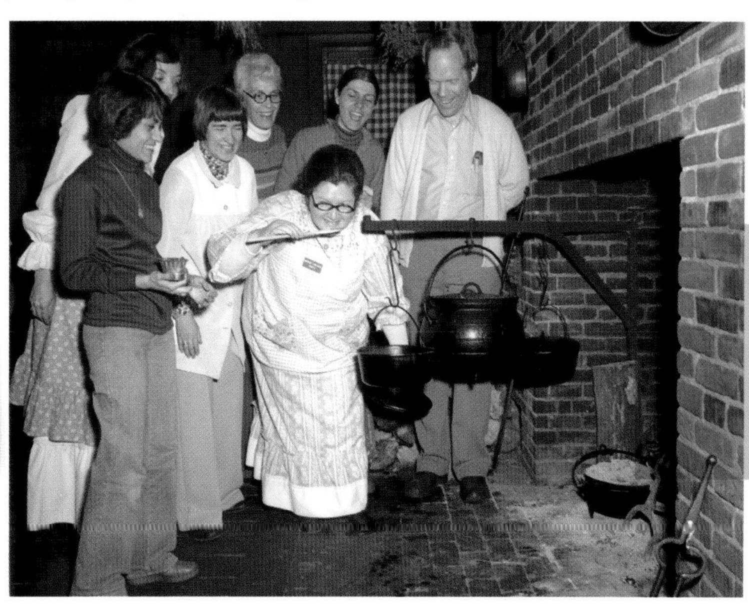

adding to the Collections

"The Edison Institute maintains one of the most active, cooperative programs in the country for Americana enthusiasts."

– *Selected Treasures of Greenfield Village and Henry Ford Museum*, 1969

With an unmatched treasury of America's past already at their fingertips, the staff at Henry Ford Museum continued Henry Ford's vision as they began to add to the collection.

In the mid-1950s through to the 1980s, the institution received a number of significant artifacts. The Allegheny locomotive, one of the largest and most photographed museum artifacts, arrived at Henry Ford Museum in 1956. After eighteen days of effort, the six-hundred-ton 1941 Allegheny locomotive just barely eased into its spot on the museum's back floor.

In 1964, the institution received a significant acquisition: the Ford Motor Company Archives, one of the most extensive records of a multinational corporation in existence. Containing millions of letters, documents, photographs, advertising, oral histories, and other materials, the vast collection offered an unparalleled look at the history of the company as well as the life of its founder, Henry Ford.

The Archives moved into remodeled office space located in the upper floors of the museum building, where it was visited by a steady stream of scholars, Ford Motor Company staff, and other researchers. Several years later, the Ford Motor Company fund awarded $500,000 to create an expanded archival facility in the former school gymnasium in Lovett Hall.

In 1974, North Central Airlines donated a 1939 DC-3 Douglas airplane that, at the time of its donation, had flown more than eighty-five thousand hours, more than any other plane. In 1978, the Ford Motor Company donated the limousine President and Mrs. John F. Kennedy rode in when he was assassinated in Dallas, Texas, in 1963. The car, leased by the government from Ford Motor Company, was extensively rebuilt and then used by four presidents after Kennedy. The Ford Motor Company donation stipulated that the car could not be displayed until the Kennedy children reached adulthood.

In the 1970s, museum staff began to place more emphasis on collecting decorative and fine arts, such as furniture and paintings.

(Top) Stylish and rare, the 1930 Bugatti Royale came to the museum in 1958.

(Bottom) Paul Revere was best known as an American patriot. He was also a silversmith and engraver. One of his most famous political engravings was his depiction of the Boston Massacre of March 1770, pictured here.

(Opposite) Parts of the engine had to be removed and the museum doors had to be enlarged to fit the Allegheny locomotive into the museum.

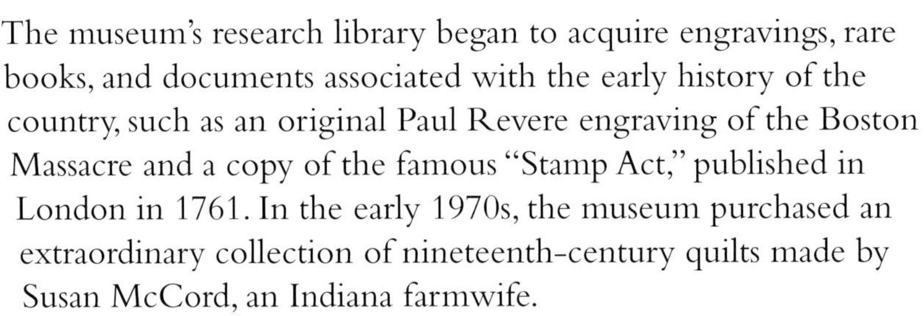

The museum's research library began to acquire engravings, rare books, and documents associated with the early history of the country, such as an original Paul Revere engraving of the Boston Massacre and a copy of the famous "Stamp Act," published in London in 1761. In the early 1970s, the museum purchased an extraordinary collection of nineteenth-century quilts made by Susan McCord, an Indiana farmwife.

Fine cabinetry of colonial craftsmen, gaily painted furniture of the Pennsylvania Germans, colorful porcelain tableware, and folk art paintings by famous artists increasingly joined the museum's world-class collections.

(Above) Susan McCord was an Indiana farmwife and quilter with an extraordinary eye. This is a variation of a crazy quilt pattern called "Fan."

(Right) After landing at the Ford test track, the DC-3 airplane was moved by truck to the museum across the street.

A Famous Fake

A search for early American furniture led the museum to the now notorious Brewster chair.

When the Brewster chair was acquired in 1970, it was thought to be a rare example of furniture from the 1600s. Seven years later, a newspaper article told of an expert woodworker who had meticulously crafted and "aged" such a chair, in an attempt to fool the experts. An extensive analysis proved the museum's chair was indeed this modern, and now infamous, fake.

The Brewster chair, a "famous fake," was acquired in 1970 and revealed as a forgery seven years later.

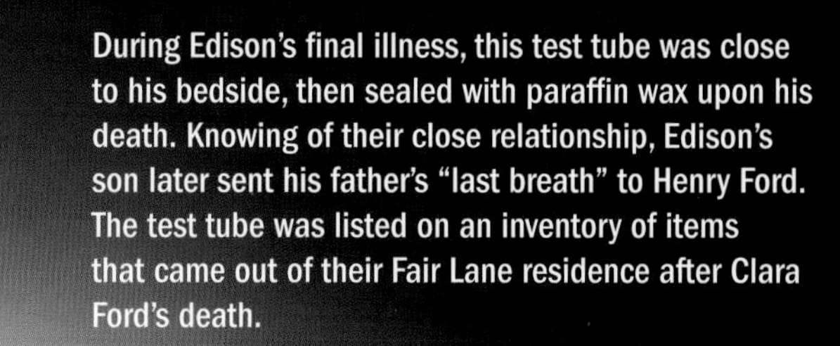

During Edison's final illness, this test tube was close to his bedside, then sealed with paraffin wax upon his death. Knowing of their close relationship, Edison's son later sent his father's "last breath" to Henry Ford. The test tube was listed on an inventory of items that came out of their Fair Lane residence after Clara Ford's death.

FACT:

Henry and Clara Ford saved everything. After Clara's death in 1950, company officials found an unexpected treasure trove of letters, receipts, and photographs at the Fords' home.

(Above) One of a series of eight Norman Rockwell paintings commissioned by Ford Motor Company to commemorate their fiftieth anniversary in 1953. The company's 1964 donation of its historical archives includes three of the Rockwell paintings, including this scene of a "Model T on the Farm."

(Left) The Ford Archives included a wealth of personal Ford family materials and Ford Motor Company business records.

After John F. Kennedy was assassinated in this car in Dallas, Texas, in 1963, it was extensively rebuilt and used by the White House until 1977. Built as a convertible, it became a closed car with a bulletproof body and bulletproof glass.

TEXACO
WELCOME
THEATRE

expansion and Renewal

"We must realize that the area in which we operate–the attraction of visitors–has become extremely competitive in recent years . . . A major purpose of our development program is to add the means by which we can offer visitors a greater sense of personal participation–all within a historical context."

– **William Clay Ford, Chairman of the Board,** ***Greenfield Villager*****, July 1972**

In 1969, as the institution celebrated its fortieth anniversary, William Clay Ford, then board chairman of Henry Ford Museum and Greenfield Village, announced that both the Ford Motor Company and the Ford Foundation would each donate $20 million in grants to the organization.

In speaking at the anniversary celebration that year, William Clay Ford said, "I think the institute is one of the great philanthropic legacies of my grandfather. It in no way diminishes the significance of this historic resource to note that he underestimated its financial needs when he conceived it more than a generation ago."

Nearly half of the money was used for needed improvements to museum and village facilities and programming. The remainder was used to create an endowment fund to provide for future income. The announcement launched a period of development not seen since Henry Ford's era.

The 1970s witnessed a flurry of planning and construction, with a steady stream of improvements designed to broaden the appeal and educational impact of Henry Ford Museum and Greenfield Village. Attendance at historic sites was climbing during the early 1970s as the nation moved toward the bicentennial of its founding. The expansion was intended to attract new audiences and set the institution on a path to self-sufficiency.

In Greenfield Village, the most dramatic changes were the new railroad and period amusement park. The railroad line, completed in 1972, circled the village perimeter. Visitors rode in open cars, pulled by a steam locomotive. The train quickly became a visitor favorite.

Museum President Donald Shelley and Chairman of the Board William Clay Ford drove in golden spikes to complete the new railroad line in August 1972.

(Opposite) The museum acquired the 1873 Torch Lake locomotive to use on the new Greenfield Village railroad tracks.

FACT:
A horse-drawn trolley and nickelodeon theater were among the original ideas proposed for the Suwanee Park complex but were not implemented.

(Right) The new gift shop near the entrance to Greenfield Village resembled a row of old storefronts.

(Below right) A new Village Craft Center, which opened in 1975, gathered the broom making, pottery, tin ware, coopering, and other craft demonstrations into one area.

(Below) An overview of Suwanee Park.

Suwanee Park, located alongside the Suwanee Lagoon, opened in 1974 as a re-creation of a turn-of-the-twentieth-century amusement park. The complex was designed to be a "focal point of fun," offering "a nostalgic look at how Americans amused themselves in bygone days." The centerpiece of the new amusement park complex was a restored, fully operational, 1913 Herschell-Spillman Carousel.

(Above) The Daggett Farmhouse in Greenfield Village.

The village received an important new building in the 1970s, a mid-eighteenth-century rural Connecticut saltbox house (now Daggett Farmhouse). In 1951, antiquarian Mary Dana Wells disassembled the house and moved it thirty-five miles from Andover to Union, Connecticut. She restored the house and lived in it until she donated it to Greenfield Village in 1977.

In Henry Ford Museum, the vast Hall of Technology (now the William Clay Ford Hall of American Innovation) underwent a total redesign. A new Interpretive Center helped visitors understand the ways that technology had shaped American life over three hundred years. Two new galleries, created by enclosing museum courtyards, offered

(Below) The centerpiece of Suwanee Park was a 1913 Herschell-Spillman Carousel.

(Right) A visitor took this shot of flames surging across the museum floor.

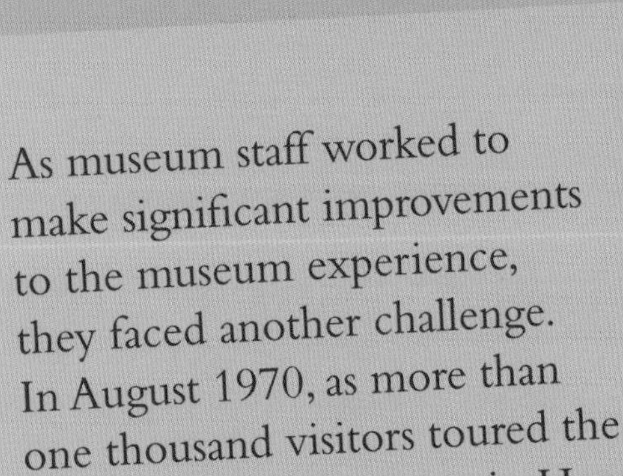

As museum staff worked to make significant improvements to the museum experience, they faced another challenge. In August 1970, as more than one thousand visitors toured the exhibits, a fire broke out in Henry Ford Museum. Thirty Dearborn firefighters quickly arrived on the scene to fight the raging blaze. By the time the blaze was brought under control an hour later, an acre of museum exhibits had been turned into rubble.

It was one of the worst fires ever to hit an American museum, destroying hundreds of artifacts, including major portions of the textile collections. Charred bits of agricultural equipment, hand tools, pottery, stoves, mirrors, musical instruments, and books lay scattered among the smoldering ruins.

Though the museum reopened to the public in just two days, it was a full year before the building was completely repaired, the teakwood floor replaced, and all the exhibits cleaned or rebuilt.

Damaged cigar store Indians, weathervanes, and other museum objects stand in eerie silhouette with the destruction of the fire around them.

(Above left) The Home Arts exhibit included a set of period kitchens. This is the 1930s kitchen.

(Above right) The new music gallery housed the museum's fine collection of American-made musical instruments.

additional space to showcase the museum's collections. The rows of cars, spinning wheels, tractors and other technology displays were made more understandable with the use of color-coded carpet, uniform label styles, and fewer objects on display. A set of period kitchens in the Home Arts area put the collections of household equipment in historical context and was a popular addition.

New restaurants and gift shops further improved the visitor experience. Heritage Hall, a two-story restaurant adjoining the museum on the east side, opened in 1974, replacing the old Garden Room. Heritage Hall offered visitors a choice of cafeteria-style dining or table service. A new gift shop, located near the Gatehouse entrance to Greenfield Village, was built to resemble a row of old storefronts.

In 1972, the museum opened its first professional conservation lab and staffed it with trained conservators.

A year later, the Tannahill Research Library (now incorporated into the Benson Ford Research Center) opened and held the institution's remarkable collection of historical manuscripts, books, periodicals, maps, prints, photographs, music, and graphic collections. The new library brought these collections together and made them available for research.

(Below) A former racquetball court in the Education Building (now Lovett Hall) became the Tannahill Research Library in 1973.

TRANSPORTATION

(Above) The Interpretive Center provided an introduction to the history of American technology.

(Right) A detail of the exhibit.

(Opposite) The newly reorganized Transportation exhibit.

celebrating the American Bicentennial

"Liberty is a living flame to be fed, not dead ashes to be revered, even in a Bicentennial Year."

– President Gerald R. Ford, Bicentennial Celebration, Philadelphia, July 4, 1976

The Bicentennial of American Independence in 1976 was a major cultural phenomenon.

For more than a year, it seemed that everyone—from small towns to big cities—was organizing events and activities to commemorate this milestone.

The U.S. Treasury issued special Bicentennial-themed coinage; the postal service issued commemorative stamps; a Freedom Train crossed the country. A distinctive star emblem graced the official Bicentennial flag, which flew everywhere. As a wave of patriotism and nostalgia swept the nation, people wore red, white, and blue clothing and painted their mailboxes with patriotic symbols, and hundreds of commercial products were marketed in Bicentennial-themed packages.

The Bicentennial heightened Americans' interest in their history. Museums and historical sites all across the nation developed new programming to meet the needs of people looking to celebrate two hundred years of American history. Greenfield Village and Henry Ford Museum was no exception.

The guiding staff donned red, white, and blue uniforms in celebration of the Bicentennial.

(Opposite) *The Struggle and the Glory* exhibition told the story of America's transition from British colony to independent nation.

The museum and village launched its own vigorous calendar of Bicentennial activities, exhibits, and events. A special exhibit, *The Struggle and the Glory*, included more than 250 Revolutionary-period maps, prints, letters, and objects that told the story of America's struggle to become an independent nation. In this exhibit, visitors got a close-up look at an original Paul Revere engraving of the 1770 Boston Massacre. They gazed at letters written by General George Washington and saw the camp bed he slept in during the latter part of the Revolutionary War. Concerts, plays, lectures, and movies throughout the year also highlighted American historical events, characters, and musical development.

FACT:
Bicentennial fever encouraged high visitation. The museum and village saw a record attendance of 1.75 million that year.

The apex of festivities occurred on the July Fourth weekend with the presentation of a rich slate of Revolutionary War–era activities. For three days, costumed re-enactors demonstrated military maneuvers and period crafts; musicians played fife and drum concerts. A special "Let Freedom Ring" ceremony took place in front of the museum entrance, a replica of Philadelphia's Independence Hall. Thirty-five members of an antique bicycle club, the League of American Wheelmen, mounted their bikes and set off for a thirteen-day trek to Philadelphia's Independence Hall.

At 2:00 p.m. on the Fourth of July, bells rang out in communities nationwide. As four thousand people gathered in front of Henry Ford Museum, the replica of the Liberty Bell in the museum's clock tower pealed along with thousands of other bells across the nation.

(Left) Costumed Revolutionary War re-enactors paraded in front of the museum in July 1976.

(Right) A "Calendar of Bicentennial Events" for Greenfield Village and Henry Ford Museum featured the logos of the American Revolution Bicentennial and the Michigan Bicentennial Commission (lower left and right).

CHAPTER 3

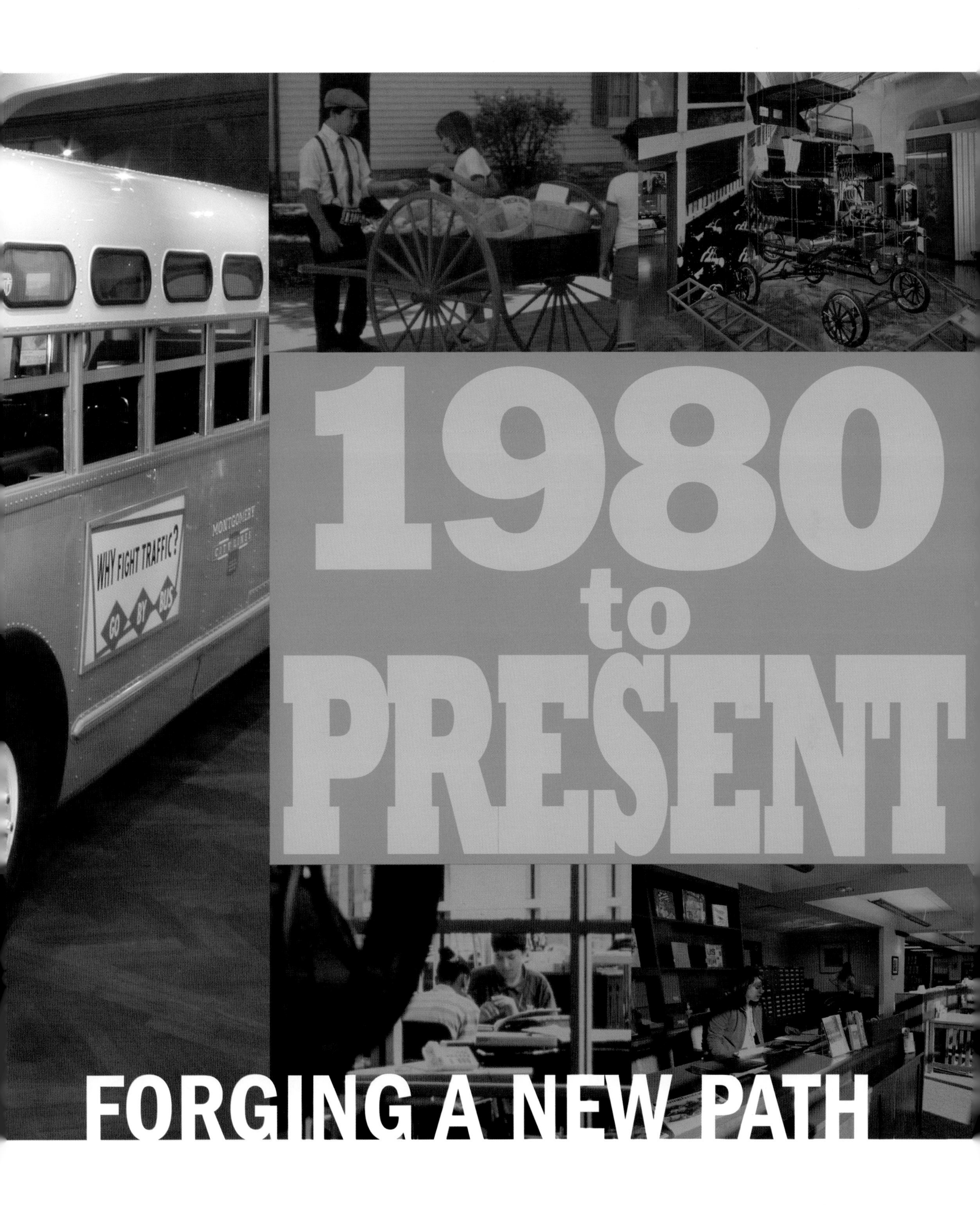

1980 to PRESENT

FORGING A NEW PATH

identifying the Need for Change

"It was like turning on a faucet around this place. Things began to happen."

– Anonymous Employee, 1982

After the record attendance of the 1976 Bicentennial, the museum's attendance in the early 1980s began to decline as Americans tired of "Bicentennial-mania" and Michigan's automotive-based economy started to spiral downward.

> "The Ford Museum is still . . . marching to the beat of its own drummer, and a frustrating, woeful example of missed opportunity."
>
> – Larry Lankton, *Technology and Culture*, October 1980

Henry Ford Museum & Greenfield Village reached its low point with 1982's attendance of 956,000, putting the organization's very survival in question.

In 1980, museum president Frank Caddy announced his retirement. Frank Caddy was one of the last of the generation that had worked for "Mr. Ford." He was a student at the Henry Ford Trade School when Henry Ford selected him to work in Greenfield Village. He slowly moved up the ranks until he became president in 1976, a position he held for four years. The Board of Trustees, encouraged by its youngest member, Sheila Ford, decided to find a new president with a national search. Their search led them to Harold K. Skramstad Jr., who was then director of the Chicago Historical Society. Skramstad had a PhD in American Civilization and experience at the Smithsonian's National Museum of American History. Only forty-one years old, he was part of a new generation of social historians, intent upon conveying the importance of common, everyday history to a broad public audience.

Board chairman William Clay Ford (left) and trustees Sheila Ford and Lynn Alandt with president Frank Caddy at the opening of the Interpretive Center in 1979. In 1989 William Clay Ford stepped down from thirty-eight years of board leadership to become chairman emeritus. His daughter Sheila Ford Hamp became the first woman and the first of her generation to chair the museum's board of trustees.

(Opposite) The Innovation Station, a giant participatory "activity center" created in Henry Ford Museum in 1992, embodied the new mission focus on innovation.

Skramstad took the reins of the institution and immediately made some changes. He trimmed the staff by 30 percent and instituted new financial controls. He doubled the admission fee, began a comprehensive

(Above) In charting a new course for the institution, Skramstad relied on the measure of "money, market, and mission" to evaluate what programs should go and what should stay.

development program with an annual giving campaign, and broadened the membership program. He sold the Dearborn Inn to increase the endowment and diversified the endowment portfolio to include more than just Ford stock. Building a persuasive case around the museum's "world-class" collections, he found new sources of financial support, successfully tapping in to the National Endowment for the Humanities and private foundations in ways unprecedented for the museum.

By the mid-1980s, the place was turning around and the staff was infused with a "spirit of optimism." Skramstad had succeeded in providing the organization with "a clear sense of what we are and what we must do to assure a strong future for this important American institution."

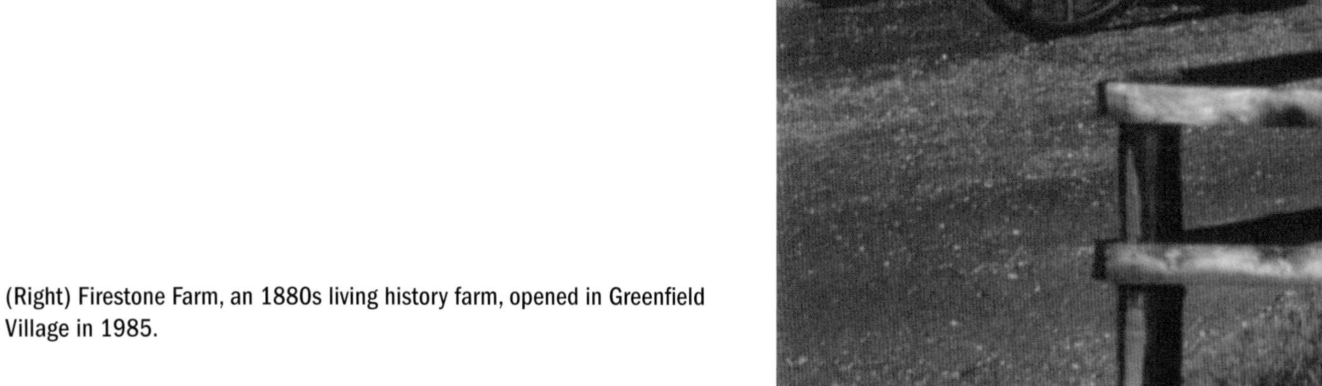

(Right) Firestone Farm, an 1880s living history farm, opened in Greenfield Village in 1985.

FACT:
One of Harold Skramstad's early ideas was to revive Henry Ford's original name for the place–The Edison Institute–as a reminder of Ford's intent to memorialize Thomas Edison's ingenuity and enterprising spirit. The name created confusion, and its public use lasted only a few years.

stories of a Changing America

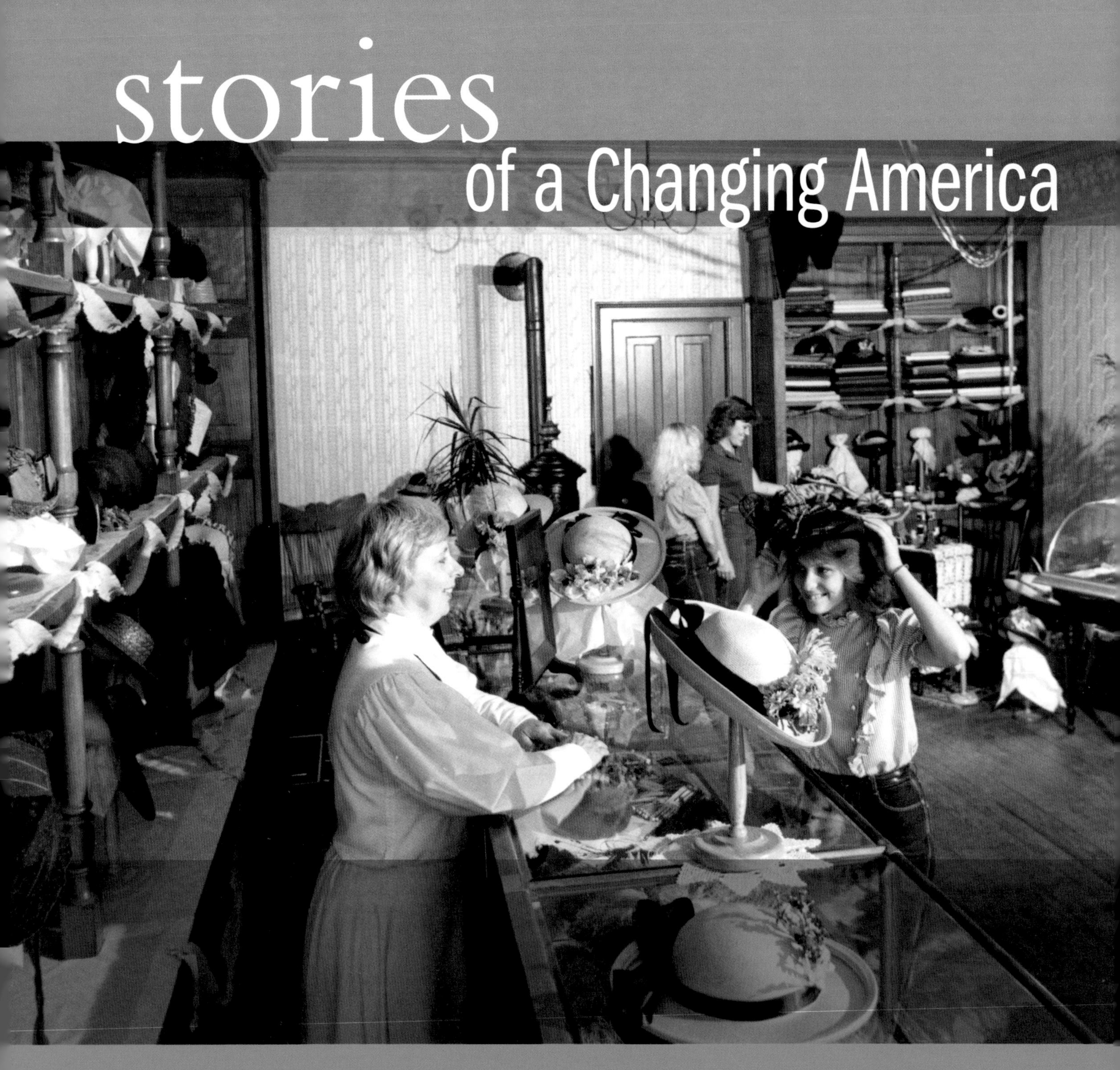

"The foundation of The Edison Institute is, of course, its collections."

– Curriculum Committee, Report, 1981

To determine the vision, purpose, and identity of the museum, Skramstad appointed a Curriculum Committee to study the existing programs and activities and make recommendations for the future.

The Curriculum Committee conducted an analysis of the strengths and weaknesses of the collections, comparing the holdings of specific types of collections to other institutional holdings.

The committee determined that sixteen areas of the collection were the finest in the country, including agricultural machinery, automobiles, bicycles, and steam engines. An additional ten collecting areas—including furniture, household appliances, and telephone equipment—were the second or third best of their kind.

The committee concluded that "It is . . . the modernization of America in general and technology and its effects in particular that constitute the core curriculum of the Edison Institute." The museum's unique strength was its ability to demonstrate America's evolution from a rural, pre-industrial society to an urban, industrial nation.

At the Connecticut Saltbox House (now called Daggett Farmhouse), interpreters in period clothing re-created the activities of a rural household of the 1760s.

(Opposite) As a result of more up-to-date research, the former Magill Jewelry shop reemerged as Cohen's Millinery, complete with period hats for visitors to try on.

The Curriculum Committee's important work led to the museum's first mission statement—focusing on the process of change in America, with an emphasis on the period of greatest change, 1840 to 1950.

Curators set to work, uncovering stories of change that provided the framework for new, re-envisioned, and reinterpreted buildings in Greenfield Village. Rather than being fixed in a particular place and time—like Colonial Williamsburg—the village "jumped from scene to scene" like a movie. Together the "scenes" re-created a larger picture of America's changing past.

Family letters, written reminiscences, and household inventories revealed new insights about Noah Webster's house. When the home reopened to the public in 1988, it had been transformed to reflect the activities of the family members who lived there. Webster's study included a writing table and several hundred books, similar to ones he had owned, lining the wall.

Evolution of a Mission Statement

The mission statement from 1982 characterized the museum's purpose as one of collecting and storytelling:

> *Henry Ford Museum & Greenfield Village has as its mission to collect, preserve, and interpret to a broad public audience the American historical experience with a special emphasis on the relationship between technological change and American history.*

Ten years later in 1992, a revised mission statement highlighted America's history of ingenuity, resourcefulness, and innovation as a way to encourage social activism. The Henry Ford continues to draw inspiration from this mission statement:

> *The Henry Ford provides unique educational experiences based on authentic objects, stories, and lives from America's traditions of ingenuity, resourcefulness, and innovation. Our purpose is to inspire people to learn from these traditions to help shape a better future.*

To create a more historically accurate setting at Menlo Park Laboratory, staff filled the laboratory shelves with more than two thousand bottles of chemicals like those that Edison had kept on hand for experiments.

FACT:
In contradiction to a programmatic emphasis on the colonial era, the Curriculum Committee found that 85 percent of the museum's collections and most of the buildings in Greenfield Village fell within the period 1800 to 1950.

“activation”

“The activation of a number of our structures has . . . been a top priority.”

– Steven K. Hamp, Annual Report, 1981–82

Armed with the new mission statement, a task force of curators, educators, and interpreters explored ways to make the stories of a changing America come alive in Greenfield Village and in new special events in Henry Ford Museum.

FACT:
The circular sawmill produced so many boards of lumber that museum staff began using them for village building restoration projects.

The noise and movement of historic machinery began to fill Greenfield Village. The deafening buzz of the steam-powered saw and the pungent smell of freshly created sawdust heightened the experience for visitors to the circular sawmill, reactivated in Greenfield Village during the summer of 1981.

"Activation" was the word of the day as dormant buildings and machinery—some operational during Henry Ford's time—came back to life. Greenfield Village was filled with activity as staff demonstrated long-forgotten farm tasks and obsolete industrial skills, and encouraged visitors to participate.

A cohesive interpretive staff was created from the previous groups of guides, crafts people, and village ride attendants. A period clothing program, grounded in historical research, further enlivened village interpretation.

New programs, aligned with the mission statement and grounded in solid historical research, offered audiences a chance to participate in special events that suited their interests. Greenfield Village's Halloween program, for example, began in 1981 as a one-night family program featuring ghosts of Greenfield Village characters. Discovery Camp, an unusual program for its time, offered young children the opportunity to learn from and participate in museum and village activities during the summer months.

In 1986, Henry Ford Museum & Greenfield Village added a second car show, Motor Muster, which featured newer cars than Old Car Festival (first presented in 1951). Henry Ford Museum became the site of the popular Great Escape weekends, which invited visitors to immerse themselves in the leisure-time activities and popular culture of previous decades.

(Opposite) The Armington & Sims Machine Shop, a reproduction of a typical small machine shop of the 1890s, was reactivated in the summer of 1982. During breathtaking demonstrations of the foundry, visitors could watch red-hot, molten iron poured into sand molds to cool and harden—re-creating the process of how cast iron products were made during the late 1800s.

(Above) The Games on the Green program enlivened the village green by involving visitors in such turn-of-the-century outdoor pastimes as stilt walking and hoop rolling.

Food had never been viewed as more than a visitor amenity. Now it was seen as part of the interpretive experience. The Covered Bridge lunch stand began selling turn-of-the-century picnic lunches. Vendors hawked fruit and penny candy from rolling carts. The Owl Night Lunch wagon was authentically restored and offered refreshments during the summer months in Greenfield Village.

Eagle Tavern was the food program's "crown jewel." The Clinton, Michigan, inn had been known as the Eagle Tavern during the period that it was a stagecoach stop for travelers on the Detroit-to-Chicago road in the 1850s. The name later became the Clinton Inn. In the early 1980s, the restaurant was transformed into a historic dining experience representing the 1850s, with live presentations and period furnishings, as well as historic food, drinks, and menus. The name was changed from Clinton Inn to Eagle Tavern, the name in use in the 1850s. The popularity of Eagle Tavern inspired the creation of additional historic and immersive food experiences.

(Right) The transformed Eagle Tavern, complete with a new sign and staff in 1850s period clothing, was featured in this issue of the *Henry Ford Museum & Greenfield Village Herald.*

(Below) The Halloween program was initially marketed to members as a safe family alternative to neighborhood trick-or-treating.

Tricks and treats
for fearless families

SCARE UP SOME FUN AT OUR HALLOWEEN JAMBOREE

Here in a secure setting, families may enjoy hay wagon rides down darkened lanes, among the ghosts of Greenfield Village. Ghost stories and witch tales for the kids. Halloween treats that you help make yourself. Traditional Halloween games and contests.

Come dressed up as your favorite character from American history, you can join the big parade down pumpkin-lighted paths and enter the historic costume judging contest. Prizes, too!

This is an exciting new family event, celebrating Halloween in the community fashion of many years past.

Reservations by telephone and your credit card number. Call 271-1620, extension 452.

Children $7 each
Accompanying parents free
(Minimum of 1 adult for 4 children)

FRIDAY EVENING, OCT. 30, 6-9 PM

THE EDISON INSTITUTE
Henry Ford Museum & Greenfield Village
Dearborn, Michigan 48121

"Our visitors step back into the 1850s when they cross the threshold of our roadside tavern."

- Harold Skramstad Jr., letter to members, 1982

Children in the Discovery Camp program worked the fields of Firestone Farm in the summer of 1985.

(Below) From 1983 to 1986, the Great Escape Weekends in Henry Ford Museum immersed visitors in leisure and entertainment activities of specific decades, like this lively 1920s dance performance.

(Right) Street vendors added atmosphere and activity to Greenfield Village streets while also giving visitors the chance to take a break with some light refreshment.

(Below) The Owl Night Lunch wagon, the last known surviving lunch wagon of its type, was restored to its former appearance at the turn of the twentieth century, when workers like Henry Ford frequented it in downtown Detroit.

Henry Ford Museum
& Greenfield Village
presents

Motor Muster
August 9-10,
1986

Great cars from 1930 through 1959 will be the centerpiece of the newest village fun-filled weekend!

The Great American Museum
That's Also Great Fun!
Dearborn, Michigan

(Right) The Motor Muster car show features cars that are at least twenty-five years old.

FACT:
The long tubes of macaroni, served with many of the beverages at Eagle Tavern, came from research into historical drinking habits. Some drinks, it turned out, were typically served with "suckers"—made of straw (from which our modern term derives), silver, glass, or macaroni!

(Left) A re-created Chautauqua tent in Greenfield Village in 1984 and 1985 featured a variety of performances similar to those that uplifted and enlightened audiences just before World War I.

(Below left) In 1993, the Detroit Symphony Orchestra and Henry Ford Museum & Greenfield Village partnered to create the "Salute to America" concerts. The series of concerts, held in Greenfield Village around the Fourth of July holiday, have become a much-anticipated annual event.

(Below) This eye-catching clock provided a focal point at the new Taste of History restaurant in Greenfield Village (1994)—complete with moving fork-and-knife hands and a working miniature train that encircled it. Behind the clock were large murals of agricultural scenes made of Indian corn, inspired by those at the famed Corn Palace in Mitchell, South Dakota. The menu allowed visitors to experience updated versions of some classic regional foods.

firestone Farm

Firestone Farm will be "a working, living, historical farm where one can see, feel, smell, hear and participate in yesteryear."

– Peter Cousins, Curator of Agriculture, 1985

Henry Ford and Harvey Firestone, founder of the Firestone Tire and Rubber Company, were great friends and business associates.

In 1983, the Firestone family donated the 1828 farmstead (the home, barn, springhouse, and their contents) that had been Harvey's childhood home. This extensive addition to Greenfield Village provided an opportunity to create a completely immersive, year-round authentic farm experience for visitors. The Firestone Farm allowed the staff to take the concept of "activation" to a more sophisticated level.

First, the farmhouse and large "bank" barn had to be documented, dismantled, and moved from Columbiana in southeastern Ohio. Meticulous research guided decisions on how to reconstruct the house and barn, as well as how to furnish it, what kind of livestock to acquire, what crops to plant, and how to develop daily programs based on the Firestone family's activities during the 1880s.

On June 29, 1985, former U.S. President Gerald R. Ford dedicated the newly installed Firestone Farm in Greenfield Village. Two of Harvey's sons, Raymond C. and Leonard K. Firestone, his granddaughter Martha Firestone Ford, and other members of the Firestone family contributed to the financial support for this complicated undertaking.

When the Firestone Farm opened to the public, the complex included the barn and outbuildings, gardens and orchards, field crops, and grazing pastures. The farm stock even included wrinkly Merino sheep, popular in the 1800s for the many layers of wool they yielded for sale, as well as other heritage animal breeds. The farm staff, dressed in typical late-nineteenth-century farm clothes, performed daily and seasonal chores, just as the Firestones might have done a hundred years earlier.

(Top right) Former President Gerald Ford and Harold Skramstad at the dedication of Firestone Farm in Greenfield Village, June 1985.

(Above) A handwritten note with young Harvey's signature, found while removing a section of ceiling above the central stairway, was a clue to documenting the 1882 house renovation.

(Opposite) The Firestone house on its original site, just before the 1882 renovation (young Harvey is second from right). The farmhouse was dismantled brick by brick in 1984 and moved to Greenfield Village, along with a large barn

FACT:
Henry Ford and Harvey Firestone were longtime friends. From 1918 to 1924, Ford and Firestone went camping together every summer as part of the "vagabonds," a group that included Thomas Edison, naturalist John Burroughs, and famous guests such as President Warren G. Harding, who joined them in the summer of 1921.

(Above) The Firestone farmhouse nears completion on its new site in Greenfield Village.

(Right) When the Firestone family renovated their home in 1882, they updated their parlor with stylish furnishings, colors, and patterns. This is the parlor in the restored farmhouse.

FACT:

In 1947, Henry Ford's grandson William Clay Ford married Harvey Firestone's granddaughter Martha Firestone.

(Above left and below) Daily and seasonal chores on the farm were based on research into typical 1880s farming activities for eastern Ohio.

exhibits

Explore New Topics

"Visitors and reviewers alike should not lose sight of the radical change this exhibit brings to the Henry Ford Museum."

– Charles K. Hyde, exhibit review of *Automobile in American Life, Technology and Culture*, 1989

By the mid-1980s, the addition of Firestone Farm, new interpretive building installations, and the operation of historic mills and machinery created a new visitor experience in Greenfield Village.

Changing the museum exhibits to reflect the new mission statement and the new emphasis on social history proved harder to accomplish. The museum retained much of the typological display approach of Henry Ford's day. The only attempt to place museum objects into a historical context, the Interpretive Center, had been installed in 1979 for the museum's fiftieth anniversary, but it didn't last long. The large displays of categories of objects remained for some time.

Over the next several years, museum staff explored a number of smaller topics that integrated different collections.

Mass-Produced Elegance, the first of the new interpretive exhibits, drew on the strengths of the collections to explore how mass production brought goods to a growing number of middle-class Americans between 1830 and 1910. *Streamlining America* examined the design style that influenced almost every aspect of American life from the mid-1930s through the 1950s and was accompanied by a handsome catalogue, a first for the museum.

Streamlining America included this dramatically designed store window, modeled after Lord & Taylor's 1941 display window in New York City.

(Opposite) The new exhibits explored the social impact of technology, including the development of roadside culture—motels, drive-ins, and gas stations.

The most visible coming of age of the new generation of public presentations was the *Automobile in American Life*, a 50,000-square-foot exhibition in the museum that opened in 1987 and examined how the automobile changed Americans' way of life. The new design—vastly different from the former "parking lot" display—combined cars, car accessories, roadside architecture, paper documents, books, photographs, banners, and media presentations in interpretive settings. An authentic ten-foot-by-fifteen-foot 1930s tourist cabin from the Irish Hills of

(Above) In 1990, a new interpretive exhibit in the Heinz House in Greenfield Village featured the brand-name products and creative promotional strategies of the H. J. Heinz Company. It also provided the opportunity to highlight the museum's large collection of Heinz materials, acquired with the house in 1953.

(Right) The scale of the museum building easily accommodated large-scale architectural elements in the *Automobile in American Life*. Roadside icons, such as this early McDonald's sign, a diner, a Texaco station, a tourist cabin, and a neon drive-in theatre sign all fit comfortably inside the great hall. Taken together, they conveyed the impact of the automobile on American life.

(Below) The museum partnered with the magazine *Popular Mechanics* to create the temporary exhibit *Possible Dreams: Americans' Enthusiasm for Technology* (1992) that explored Americans' enthusiasm for technology over the last ninety years, as reflected in the pages of *Popular Mechanics* magazine. Jimmy Clark's Lotus Ford, which won the Indianapolis 500 race in 1965, was featured in the exhibit.

Michigan was juxtaposed with a room from a 1950s Holiday Inn—complete with an original neon sign. The full-sized 1946 Lamy's Diner from Marlborough, Massachusetts, was placed next to a twenty-foot-tall 1960 McDonald's sign from Sterling Heights, Michigan.

The exhibition was a hit. Attendance to Henry Ford Museum & Greenfield Village increased in 1988 to over 1.3 million as the public embraced this new display and the Society for the History of Technology awarded it a scholarly endorsement.

The renovation of the power and machinery collections into the 50,000-square-foot *Made in America* exhibition, in 1992, followed a similar style and educational approach. Between them, the *Automobile in American Life* and *Made in America* were the two largest exhibitions on single topics in the country. They were, in fact, larger than most museums.

FACT:
Between 1981 and the end of 1992, new exhibits were developed for over 115,000 square feet of the museum (about one-third of its exhibit space).

(Left) *Americans on Vacation* was the first major exhibit of this era to be specifically designed for travel to other museums.

(Below) *Made in America* (1992) explored America's shift to a mass production and mass consumption society. It was divided into "Making Things" and "Making Power." The exhibit included an "exploded" Model T, showing all of its standardized parts.

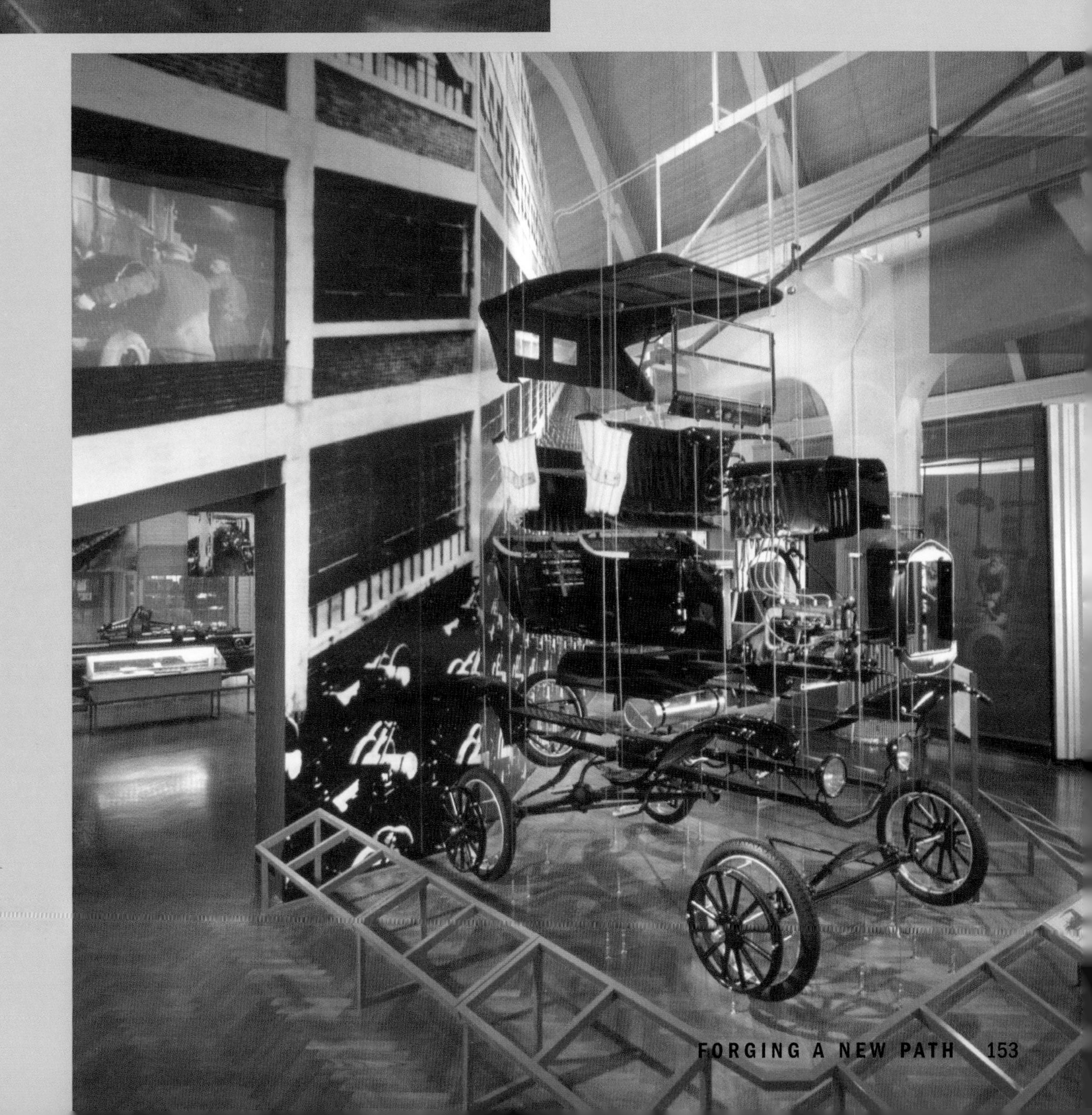

a focus on the Collections

"This is the best historical collection anywhere in the world, period."

– **Harold Skramstad Jr., *Detroit News*, July 26, 1987**

Henry Ford didn't have a collection plan or a collection policy, and he had little interest in systematic record keeping.

After Ford's death, as previously mentioned, museum staff began the arduous task of learning what the institution had. Harold Skramstad recalled that when he came to the museum he found "stuff fallin' out of closets, poppin' out of basements and stacked in back hallways."

Upon further research and with determined efforts to properly catalog the artifacts, staff came to realize that the collection was "encyclopedic" and "unparalleled."

Skramstad created a formalized program for assessing the collections and developed a process with which each curator reported to a "Collections Committee" on the strengths, gaps, and redundancies in their collections. The Committee also developed collecting guidelines for the curatorial staff as a way to build on the collection's unique strengths.

With the guidelines in place, the institution deaccessioned thousands of objects, most of them collected in Henry Ford's time, that were either duplicates or out of scope and were sold through public auction or placed with another nonprofit organization. The resulting funds were then invested in an endowment fund that supports the acquisition and care of collection items.

After the adoption of the new mission statement in 1992, curators reviewed and revised their collecting plans to focus on collecting objects and stories that reflected American ingenuity, resourcefulness, and innovation. In the late 1990s, a collections task force made several recommendations for future collecting, which included focusing on post–World War II America and increasing the racial, ethnic, and geographic diversity of the collection. The report suggested that artifacts representing social innovations should be collected along with technological innovations, always a major focus.

The cover photo of the *Detroit News* magazine (July 26, 1987) article that criticized the museum's artifact deaccessioning and sales. Other museums, such as the New-York Historical Society and the Shelburne Museum, have faced similar public criticism for their sales of deaccessioned artifacts.

(Opposite) This rare 1906 Locomobile road racer, nicknamed Old 16, won the Vanderbilt Cup in 1908 for a grueling 258-mile race—the first American automobile to win a major international competition. Paul Newman posed beside it during filming for a special museum exhibit.

(Left) An important and striking addition to the ceramics collection in 1983 was the "Jazz Bowl," designed by Viktor Schreckengost and produced around 1931 by the Cowan Pottery Company in Rocky River, Ohio.

(Below) The 1965 Moog Synthesizer, an important development in the transition from mechanical to electronic music, was a significant postwar innovation added to the museum collections in 1982.

(Above) The museum's ongoing efforts to document American product design resulted in several major acquisitions. In partnership with Herman Miller Inc., the museum created a consortium of thirteen museums to share the landmark products of Herman Miller's rich design legacy, such as George Nelson's "marshmallow" sofa.

(Above right) The Edsel Ford Design History Center, established in 1984, sponsored a project to interview automotive designers and engineers and collect automotive design drawings and other materials, such as this drawing from former General Motors design chief Bill Mitchell.

(Right) In 2000, the museum acquired a stunning collection of glass negatives by Léon Bollée, a French inventor, automobile manufacturer, and aviation enthusiast. His photographs of Wilbur Wright's 1908 flying demonstrations in France helped convince a skeptical world that flight was possible.

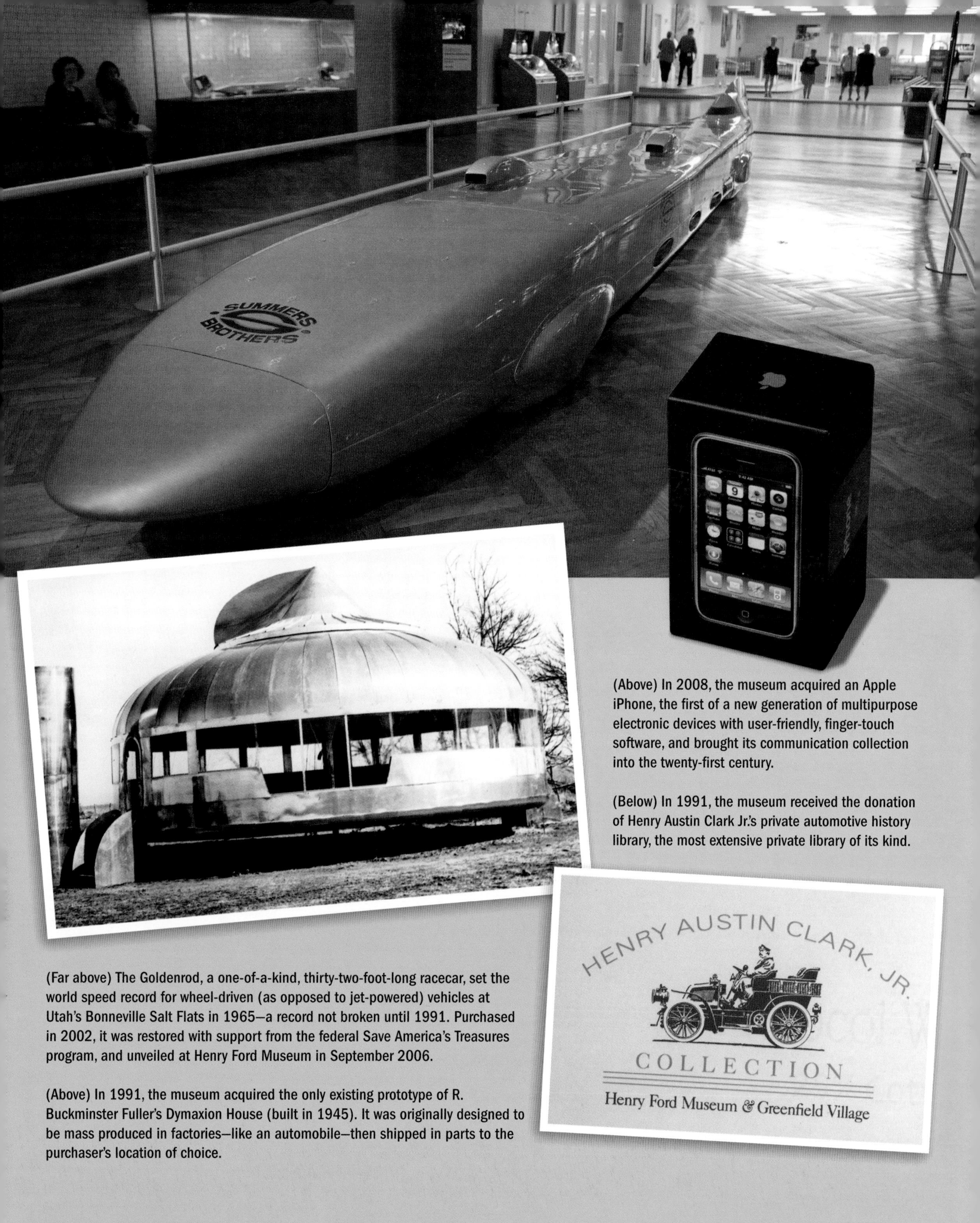

(Above) In 2008, the museum acquired an Apple iPhone, the first of a new generation of multipurpose electronic devices with user-friendly, finger-touch software, and brought its communication collection into the twenty-first century.

(Below) In 1991, the museum received the donation of Henry Austin Clark Jr.'s private automotive history library, the most extensive private library of its kind.

(Far above) The Goldenrod, a one-of-a-kind, thirty-two-foot-long racecar, set the world speed record for wheel-driven (as opposed to jet-powered) vehicles at Utah's Bonneville Salt Flats in 1965—a record not broken until 1991. Purchased in 2002, it was restored with support from the federal Save America's Treasures program, and unveiled at Henry Ford Museum in September 2006.

(Above) In 1991, the museum acquired the only existing prototype of R. Buckminster Fuller's Dymaxion House (built in 1945). It was originally designed to be mass produced in factories—like an automobile—then shipped in parts to the purchaser's location of choice.

The Rosa Parks Bus—The Beginning of the Modern Civil Rights Movement

When curators discussed how they might acquire significant artifacts to represent the key social movements of postwar America, the Montgomery, Alabama, city bus in which Rosa Parks refused to give up her seat to a white man in 1955 invariably topped the list. However, no one knew if the bus even existed. Then, in 2001, the *Wall Street Journal* reported that a bus identified as the Rosa Parks bus was being put up for auction. The bus owners had bought it from the city of Montgomery in the early 1970s. They had sold the parts and placed the bus body in a field, where time took its toll for three decades. But how could the authenticity of the bus be verified? Fortunately, the bus company manager had kept a scrapbook of clippings about Rosa Parks's arrest and the subsequent bus boycott that eventually led to the integration of Montgomery's busses. On the scrapbook's pages, the manager had recorded the name of the bus driver and the bus number, which matched the number on the bus. A museum conservator examined the bus to verify its integrity, and a forensics expert examined the scrapbook for authenticity. Convinced it was the real thing, the museum bid on the bus and the scrapbook (also for sale) and successfully acquired both for its collection. The museum had previously attempted to acquire a major civil rights icon—the Woolworth's lunch counter from Greensboro, North Carolina, that had been the site of a 1960 sit-in. However, the lunch counter went to the Smithsonian's National Museum of American History. This time, however, The Henry Ford was the winner, eventually outbidding the Smithsonian and the City of Denver, Colorado. A Save America's Treasures federal grant helped restore the bus to its appearance on that fateful day in 1955. The landmark bus is featured in the *With Liberty and Justice for All* exhibition. When Rosa Parks died in 2005, the bus was placed outside the Charles H. Wright Museum of African American History where Rosa Parks lay in honor on the day before her Detroit funeral.

ALABAMA JOURNAL --- DECEMBER 5, 1955

YCOTT CALLED EFFECTIVE:

Negress Draws Fine In Segregation Case Involving Bus Ride

(Polos On Page 5-B)

By BUNNY HONICKER

A Negro woman was fined $10 and cost in police court re today for violating a state law requiring racial segre- tion on city buses.

Rosa Parks, 634 Cleveland Ave., a seamstress at a owntown store, did not testify.

Negro Atty. Fred D. Gray informed Recorder's Court Judge John B. Scott he would appeal the decision to Montgomery Circuit Court. A few minutes later, Gray signed a $100 appeal bond for his client.

Also signing the woman's appeal bond was E. D. Nixon of Montgomery, a former state president of the National Assn. for the Advancement of Colored People.

Gray had entered a plea of innocent for his client, who stood silent throughout the hearing.

BUS DRIVER TESTIFIES

City Prosecutor Eugene Loe called Montgomery City Lines bus driver J. F. Blake to the stand to open the city's case. Blake briefly told how Rosa Parks refused to move to the rear of his bus last Thursday night after he had requested her and several others to move to make room for white passengers he was taking on near the Empire Theater.

Blake said there were 22 Negroes and 14 whites seated in the 36-seat bus and that he asked several of the Negroes to move to the rear in order to equalize the seating.

CHARGE AMENDED

At the outset, Loe moved to amend the charge against Rosa Parks, making the warrant read a violation of the state law instead of the city ordinance. Gray objected by Judge Scott allowed the amendment. The state law merely sets forth as unlawful any failure for a person to comply with the assignment or re-assignment order of a bus driver.

Gray said the law was not a city law and would not apply to his client.

Loe said the state law referred to all transportation.

Gray declined to say specifically whether the state law would be attacked as unconstitutional on appeal. But he made this suggestive comment:

"Every legal issue will be raised that I think is necessary to defend my client."

The question of constitutionality was not raised in Recorder's Court

Before and during the hearing.

(See SEGREGATION CASE, 2-A)

Segregation Case

(Continued From Page 1-A)

Judge Scott Scott shooed away photographers.

90 PER CENT BOYCOTT

The steps leading into the north side of the courtroom and the sidewalk, along with the corridors leading into the east entrance of the courtroom, all were jammed with spectators and witnesses.

Meanwhile, Montgomery City Lines Manager J. H. Bagley this afternoon estimated that some 90 per cent of the Negroes were refusing to ride the buses in protest of today's hearing.

The boycott was uncovered Saturday after thousands of unsigned circulars were reportedly being spread throughout the Negro districts in Montgomery.

ONE INCIDENT

Acting upon the orders of Police Commissioner Clyde Sellers that there was to be no violence today, patrolmen arrested a 19-year-old Negro youth who allegedly tried to restrain a Negro woman from getting on one of the morning buses.

Fred Daniel, 19, of 1646 Hall St., was jailed on a charge of disorderly conduct, according to Police Chief G. J. Ruppenthal. Arresting Patrolmen R. M. Hammonds and C. A. Weaver said Daniel grabbed a Negro woman by the arm about 7:15 a.m. at the intersection of Hall and Thurman and pulled her away from a City Lines bus she was attempting to board.

NEGRO TAXI CABS BUSY

All Negro taxi cab operators in the city reportedly told their drivers to charge only 10 cents a head today from the hours 4 a.m. to 9 a.m. and from 3 p.m. until 11 p.m. in an effort to make the bus boycott effective.

Several buses seen on downtown streets today carried nothing but white passengers from front to rear.

Several thousand Negroes use the buses on a normal day.

Police cars and motorcycles followed the buses periodically to prevent trouble after Sellers said some Negroes reported they were threatened with violence if they rode buses today.

MASS MEETING TONIGHT

A mass meeting of Negroes has also been scheduled tonight at the Holt Street Baptist Church to discuss "further instructions" in the "economic reprisal" campaign

#2857

(Above) The interior and exterior of the bus were restored to look as they did in 1955, when Rosa Parks refused to move to the back of the bus.

(Left) The bus driver's name and the bus number recorded in the scrapbook—"Blake/2857"—helped to verify the authenticity of the bus.

(Opposite) The bus sat in an open field in Alabama for thirty years, a victim of the elements and of vandals who shot holes in the windows and caused other damage.

(Below) Mourners could see the iconic bus outside the Charles H. Wright Museum of African American History where Rosa Parks lay in honor on the day before her Detroit funeral in 2005.

representing American Diversity

"It is so beautiful. I never heard of Idlewild. And to think all this was going on right here in Michigan."

– Emily Boberg, visitor, Annual Report, 2000

Henry Ford viewed American history through the lens of his own personal experience, that of a white Protestant northerner who was born on a farm and moved to the city.

The museum's historical narrative shared that perspective.

Beginning in the 1990s, a series of new programs added multiple voices to the museum's representation of the American experience. In 1991, the institution created the African American Family Life and Culture Program that featured exhibits, live performances, and hands-on activities celebrating the lives and accomplishments of African Americans. The program included moving, restoring, and reinstalling the two slave houses in Greenfield Village that were originally from the Hermitage plantation near Savannah, Georgia.

New curatorial research revealed that the wood frame home that Henry Ford had moved from Richmond Hill, Georgia, belonged to a land-owning African American family—not a white plantation overseer, as previously believed. The reinstallation of the Mattox House featured improvised newspaper "wallpaper" like other rural southern homes of the time.

A partnership with the Motown Historical Museum led to an exhibit, *The Motown Sound: The Music and the Story*, which opened in 1995. In a nightclub setting, an inspiring multimedia presentation featured Berry Gordy, Smokey Robinson, and other Motown legends describing the Motown phenomenon and its impact on the world. The Motown partnership included training of the Motown Museum staff, and the restoration and reinstallation of the Hitsville, U.S.A. building back to its 1960s heyday when it was the center of Motown recording.

(Far above) In the 1960s, the modest Hitsville building was the center of Motown recording.

(Above) A recreated nightclub provided the setting for the introductory film for *The Motown Sound: The Music and the Story.*

(Opposite) A recreated resort clubhouse provided the setting for a song and music show modeled after the programs guests enjoyed at Idlewild, an early African American resort town in northern Michigan.

(Above) The Mattox House reinstallation used newspaper "wallpaper" that was typical of rural southern homes of the period.

(Right) A presenter at Mattox House demonstrated the family's resourceful use of local food products from southeastern Georgia.

A partnership with the Arts League of Michigan created programs and performances about the Harlem Renaissance movement of the 1920s. In 2000, the Idlewild Clubhouse in Greenfield Village created a lively stage show inspired by Idlewild, an early African American resort town in northern Michigan.

Food offerings in Greenfield Village diversified as well. The previously generic Whistle-stop Café became Mrs. Fisher's Southern Cooking, featuring popular southern dishes like fried catfish, hush puppies, and sweet potato pie. It was named for Mrs. Abby Fisher, a former slave from Mobile, Alabama, who worked as a cook and caterer in San Francisco in the late 1870s. Her cookbook, *What Mrs. Fisher Knows About Old Southern Cooking*, published in 1881, is one of the first cookbooks written by an African American.

(Above) A Celebration of Emancipation, a special weekend begun in 1991, brought to life African Americans' rich cultural heritage through music and dance, drama, storytelling, and other activities. Here presenters share a Gullah folktale with visitors.

(Left) Henry Ford moved these slave houses from Richmond Hill, Georgia, to Greenfield Village in the 1930s.

Native American events were highlighted during the 1997 and 1998 Fall Harvest Days, featuring demonstrations of crafts, dancing, drumming, and storytelling by members of regional tribes.

a new President and a Museum Makeover

"If the best thing we give is a collection of . . . irrelevant objects. . . gather them for their aesthetic purposes, or for curiosity. . . or for . . . nostalgic purposes, then this institution would fall far short of what it's capable of doing."

– Steve Hamp, *Detroit Free Press*, March 16, 1997

Steven K. Hamp began his career at the museum in 1978 as a curatorial intern.

He quickly moved into leadership positions in education, public programs, and collections.

Over the years, he played a significant role in elevating the museum's educational programs, improving its exhibitions and public programs, and bringing a new level of rigor to its collections program. When Skramstad announced his retirement in 1996, the board of trustees immediately turned to the energetic, dynamic Hamp to assume the presidency.

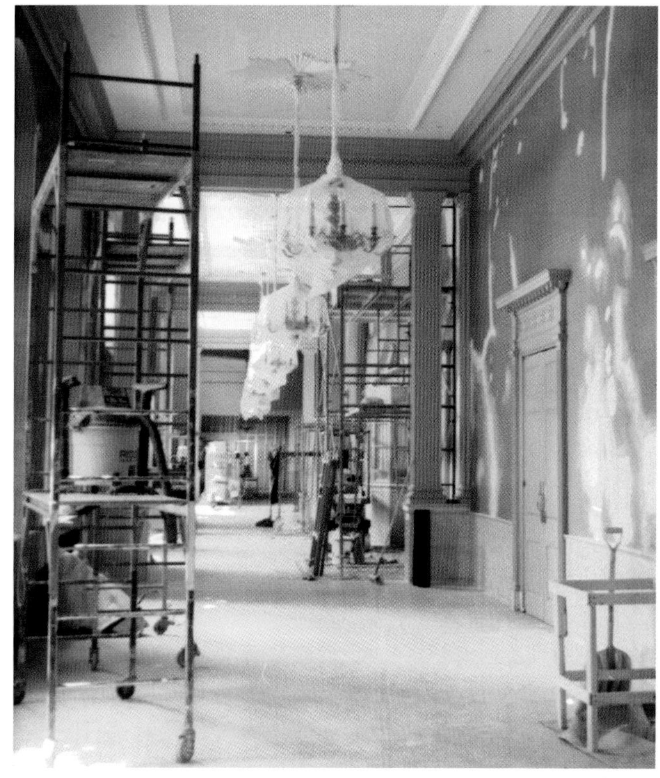

By this time, the entire campus infrastructure was badly in need of refurbishment. As president, Hamp placed an emphasis on "fit and finish" and raised the bar on the standards for all the facilities. The building housing Henry Ford Museum, however, was in the most serious state of deterioration. The structure was nearly seventy years old and had an antiquated heating system and no climate control. Signs were put out in the summer months to warn visitors about the lack of air-conditioning. Those who ventured in quickly became very uncomfortable. A warm fog formed inside during humid days, while the hot, dry winter atmosphere wreaked havoc with wooden artifacts on display. The twelve-acre roof as well as the radiator system leaked badly. Buckets to catch the drips and plastic sheeting to protect artifacts were the order of the day and a sorry sight.

Hamp announced a $40 million capital campaign—the museum's first—and funding from this and two grants from the National Endowment for the Humanities paid for a new roof, the replacement of ninety of the large original windows, and more than a mile of overhead ductwork to provide heat and air-conditioning, as well as humidity and air quality controls.

In 2000, the museum's clock tower underwent a complete restoration. In 2002, the front corridor was restored to its original grandeur with decorative painting and gilding of the elaborate plaster ceilings.

Not only did Hamp address long-term maintenance needs, but also a flurry of new construction and fund development took place during his term of office. Several major new buildings were added to the campus—the IMAX Theatre and new museum lobby, Benson Ford Research Center, and Henry Ford Academy Greenfield Village campus—along with a major new "off-campus" facility—the Ford Rouge Factory Tour—as well as the complete restoration of Greenfield Village.

(Far above) The front corridor of Henry Ford Museum, renamed the Prechter Promenade in memory of museum trustee Heinz Prechter, was restored to its former glory with decorative plastering, gilding, and painting.

(Above) A giant crane, one of the largest in the country, lifted four air-handling units onto the roof—each one about the size of a railroad car.

(Opposite) A beaming Steve Hamp poses by the tail fins of a 1959 Cadillac Eldorado in the *Automobile in American Life* exhibit.

As Steve Hamp and others looked on, President Bill Clinton signed the National Automobile Heritage Act of 1998, the legislation that created the MotorCities National Heritage Area.

When Steve Hamp became president in 1996, William Clay Ford Jr. became chairman of the board. Bill Ford is pictured here (left) with Steve Hamp at the dedication of Henry Ford Academy in 1997.

FACT:
William Clay Ford, youngest son of Edsel and Eleanor Ford, served The Henry Ford for over fifty years, first as trustee beginning in 1951, next as president, and then chairman of the board from 1965 to 1989 when he became chairman emeritus. In 1998, the board of trustees named the great hall of Henry Ford Museum the "William Clay Ford Hall of American Innovation."

Steve Hamp, Community Leader

For many years, Henry Ford & Greenfield Village was considered a "maverick organization." Several times larger than most museums, with an immense collection, an exhibition hall the size of multiple football fields, and an eighty-acre outdoor "village" populated with dozens of historic buildings, it often seemed and acted like an empire onto itself. As president of The Henry Ford, Steve Hamp began to change that. He reached out to key community organizations and constituents and created strong collaborative relationships. He encouraged his senior staff to do the same. He defined the value proposition for the Henry Ford and the communities it served in three ways—educational reform, economic development through cultural tourism, and community development through partnerships with diverse organizations. He was a driving force behind the creation of the Cultural Coalition of Southeastern Michigan and nurtured close relationships with the University of Michigan-Dearborn. He led collaborative efforts such as the Rouge River Gateway Partnership, a public-private initiative to clean up the Rouge River and restore the river's original oxbow, and he helped create the MotorCities National Heritage Area in 1998, an affiliate of the National Park Service. In recognition of his community leadership, Hamp was awarded an honorary doctor of laws degree from the University of Michigan-Dearborn in 2002.

FACT:
Crain's Detroit Business named Henry Ford Museum & Greenfield Village the "best-managed non-profit," December 20, 1999.

The clock tower restoration in 2000 included replacement of part of the roof, a fresh coat of paint to match the original 1929 color, re-glazed windows, and new gold leaf on the clock face.

innovations in Education

"We believe students learn best when information is presented in a variety of ways and when they see the connection between the classroom and the real world."

–Cora Christmas, Principal, Henry Ford Academy, Annual Report, 1999

Henry Ford had founded the Edison Institute as an educational institution while Greenfield Village served as the campus for the Edison Institute Schools, which eventually closed in the 1960s.

In the 1980s, new studies of how children learn seemed to bear out Henry Ford's belief in "learning by doing" and the power of experiential education as a way to motivate different kinds of learners. Museum educators began to develop a series of innovative educational programs that went far beyond the conventional self-directed field trip. With each new program, the museum deepened its involvement with educators and students.

The Time Travelers outreach program (begun in 1988) sent costumed interpreters with a trunk of objects to elementary school classrooms throughout the region to take students on an exploration into America's past.

A year later, the museum deepened its commitment to improving the classroom experience. In partnership with the University of Michigan-Dearborn, the museum developed a relationship with Woodward School, a Detroit inner-city elementary school. This partnership included regular classroom visits by curatorial and educational staff and student visits and hands-on participation in museum and village activities. For several years, the program culminated with an exhibit put on at the museum by the students. The 1992 exhibit, *'Damage' Dudes: What We Wear in '92*, showed how students' clothing expressed their

(Far above) At Woodward School in Detroit, a costumed "Time Traveler" enlightened students about housekeeping and daily life during the 1700s.

(Above) Smart Fun Field Trip promised both fun and learning for school groups. In this program, "Orville Wright" encouraged students to see how experimentation helped him and his brother develop their successful flying machine.

(Opposite) These Henry Ford Academy students are having a lesson in Lamy's Diner in the *Automobile in American Life* exhibit.

(Left) If I Had a Hammer combined lessons in geometry, history, interpersonal communication, and teamwork as students collaborated to build an eight-by-twelve-foot house in two hours on the museum floor.

(Below left) The walls separating the ninth grade academy classrooms from the rest of Henry Ford Museum contained clear glass windows—allowing both public viewing into the classrooms and encouraging students to feel a part of their unique environment.

(Below right) In 1991, thirty children from Detroit's Woodward School served one-day apprenticeships with Greenfield Village artisans. This student is learning about glassblowing.

identity and influenced what others thought of them. For the 1994 exhibit, *I Got My Ticket: Traveling Through My Family's Past*, students conducted oral interviews, borrowed artifacts, and created murals depicting aspects of the Great Migration, which brought twenty million southerners to northern cities, including many of the students' relatives.

The Youth Mentorship Program was developed in 1990, from a partnership with Wayne-Westland Community Schools, to work with "at risk" high school students. As part of the program, students were paired with a museum staff mentor who supervised their work assignment. In the first eighteen years of the program, twenty-seven of the students were able to graduate from high school, most being the first in their families to do so. In 1998, the program was recognized with awards from the President's Committee on the Arts and Humanities and the National Endowment for the Arts as well as the Institute of Museum and Library Services.

As concern over America's declining schools became a national issue in the 1990s, the museum began to seriously consider re-establishing a school on its grounds. The concept of a four-year charter high school began to take shape, particularly when the museum joined forces with two enthusiastic partners who were also committed to improving public education—Ford Motor

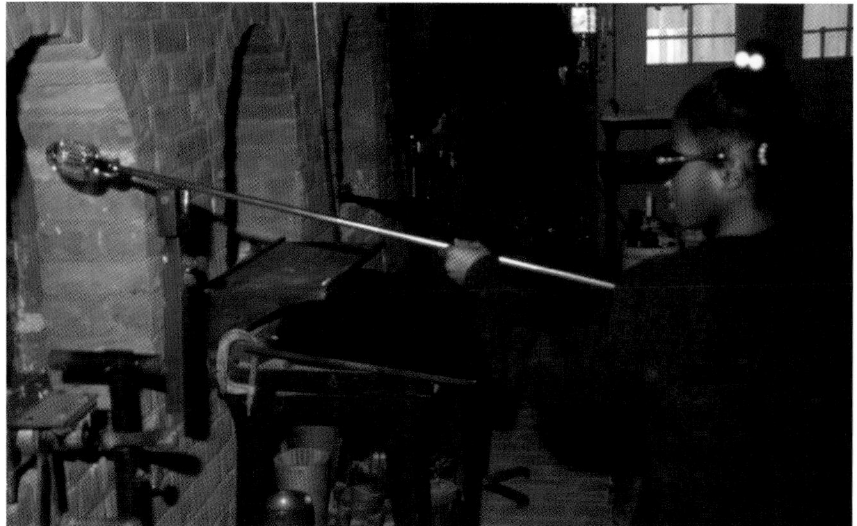

Company and the Wayne Regional Educational Service Agency. With the strong support of the museum's board of trustees, Harold Skramstad had appointed Steven K. Hamp, then director of education, to lead the efforts to establish a high school that would use the museum's objects, stories, artifacts, historic buildings, and staff expertise to create a rigorous academic, project-based, educational experience.

Henry Ford Academy opened in 1997 with one hundred freshmen who graduated in June 2001. Today, the approximately 450-member student body is one of the most diverse in Michigan. About 65 percent of the students are from Detroit, while the remaining 35 percent come from nearly thirty communities in Wayne County. Over 95 percent of the senior class graduate; over two-thirds of the graduates go on to a four-year college.

One of the goals of Henry Ford Academy was to build a replicable model that could be adopted by other community organizations and corporations. The Henry Ford Learning Institute was established in 2003 to work with community organizations to create a closely governed network of autonomous small high schools located in cultural or civic institutions—"public schools in public places." The institute's goal is to open ten new schools in communities across the country based on the Henry Ford Academy model. In August 2008, the first of these, Henry Ford Academy Power House High, opened in the North Lawndale neighborhood of Chicago, followed by two additional schools in 2009—Henry Ford Academy: Alameda School for Art + Design in San Antonio, Texas, and Henry Ford Academy: School for Creative Studies for grades 6-12 in Detroit.

Democracy on the Green, an immersive field trip program in Greenfield Village that launched in 2002, gave students a first-hand understanding of local politics as they were asked to help decide whether Greenfield Village should allow the "Mattox family" to sell their produce on the Village Green. Here Mr. and Mrs. Mattox are presenting their case to the students.

In April 2005, Microsoft founder Bill Gates, The Henry Ford's chairman Bill Ford, and its president Steve Hamp discussed the workforce of the future with about one hundred Henry Ford Academy students.

(Right) In 1998, First Lady Hillary Clinton presented Steve Hamp the National Award for Museum Service for the Youth Mentorship Program.

FACT:

The One-Room School program, offered since the 1970s, remained as popular as ever—with the addition of reproduction nineteenth-century games and an online teacher's guide.

The former Suwanee Park Train Station and other Greenfield Village buildings, as well as three vintage railroad cars, were transformed into modern classrooms for Henry Ford Academy's tenth through twelfth grades.

the next Generation of Experiences

"A history attraction uses the techniques of theater, drama, storytelling, pacing and crowd control of the themed attraction to address the important stories that matter in people's lives."

– The Henry Ford's "History Principles," 2002

As president, Steve Hamp laid out an ambitious agenda to remake Henry Ford Museum & Greenfield Village with new educational programs, improved facilities, and an accelerated drive to create a "new generation of experiences."

He adopted the theory and approach of the newly articulated "experience economy," that is, businesses that create services that are perceived as "experiences." According to experience economy theorists B. Joseph Pine II and James H. Gilmore, Starbucks doesn't just sell coffee as a commodity, it sells the "experience of coffee" and thus can charge more for it.

Visitors could watch engineers at work maintaining the steam locomotives in the reconstructed roundhouse from Marshall, Michigan, which opened to the public in 2000.

(Opposite) While researching Waterford, Michigan, for the J. R. Jones General Store, museum staff found that a spirited baseball club named the Lah-de-Dahs played there in the 1880s. When the museum started its own historic baseball club, they used the name Lah-de-Dahs. The museum added a second baseball team, the Nationals, in 2003, the year of the first World Tournament of Historic Baseball. The tournament, which was inspired by an 1867 World's Tournament of Base Ball held in Detroit, brought together eighteen historic baseball clubs from the Midwest and Canada for a weekend tournament each August. Here, a Lah-de-Dah player slugs one away.

Hamp adopted a stronger business approach to the museum's management and advocated an increased focus on earned revenue (as distinct from contributed revenue). To achieve these goals, he reorganized and began to hire senior staff and consultants who came from the business, rather than the museum, world.

In early 2000, he hired Patricia E. Mooradian as chief operating officer to oversee, develop, and connect the attractions, programs, and exhibits with contemporary audiences. Mooradian had previously worked for the Taubman Company, a real estate investment trust, headquartered in Bloomfield Hills, Michigan, that owns, develops, and operates urban and suburban shopping centers across the United States.

At the end of 1999, Hamp had presented a report to the board of trustees that proposed remaking Henry Ford Museum & Greenfield Village into a series of venues that were closely related but offered distinct and separate experiences: Henry Ford Museum, Greenfield

The Sounds of America gallery, in the Stephen Foster Memorial, took what had been a somewhat underutilized historic building and installed an exhibit that featured a portion of the museum's world-class musical instrument collections.

Village, IMAX Theatre, the Benson Ford Research Center, and Henry Ford Academy. (The Ford Rouge Factory Tour became the sixth venue in 2004.) These venues, combined with other area attractions, would create a unique, multi-day destination opportunity for local and out-of-town visitors.

This effort included the creation of a brand platform, or distinctive identity, for each of the venues and the institution as a whole. In the course of the branding initiative, it became apparent that this set of distinctive venues needed an overarching destination name that would encompass all of them. The name then currently in use, "Henry Ford Museum & Greenfield Village," no longer made sense. In January 2003, the new campus name—The Henry Ford—and the new brand platform were unveiled to the public.

The brand platform, accompanied by the newly created "History Principles," enabled staff to create a set of distinctive programmatic offerings for each venue. In Greenfield Village, special daytime programming, such as small theatrical performances and costumed strolling musicians, and new, richly produced evening events added value and character to the already highly immersive feel of the village setting.

(Right) The branding initiative led to the creation of unique logos for each of The Henry Ford's separate venues and the larger destination brand.

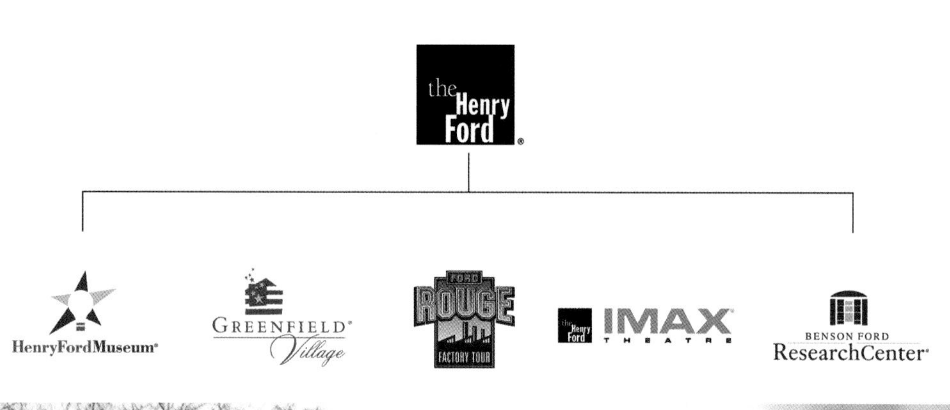

(Below) Strolling musicians, singers, and a vaudeville show in Town Hall enlivened the summer program in Greenfield Village. The "Simply Vaudeville" show entertained visitors in Town Hall in the summer of 2002.

(Right) Beginning in 2002, the "Day Out with Thomas" program brought a full-size steam locomotive to Greenfield Village for a ten-day period. The museum's own locomotives were taken out of service to allow families with young children to experience a ride with the "real" Thomas the Tank Engine on the Greenfield Village tracks.

(Above) The 12 Nights of Christmas event began rather simply in 2000 as an evening Greenfield Village program. The program became more popular as more program elements were added, such as music, strolling costumed staff, campfires, a skating rink, and themed food and shopping. The resulting Holiday Nights in Greenfield Village program was so immersive and atmospheric that it felt like stepping into a Christmas card from the past.

(Above) Tea at Cotswold Cottage (begun in summer 2004) revived the experience of afternoon tea, a favorite activity of Clara Ford and her friends during the 1920s.

The Hallowe'en program, which began in 1981, was initially a one-night event for members. Twenty years later, Hallowe'en in Greenfield Village was a public program offered for ten nights in October. The thousands of families who participated experienced a village transformed by elaborate costumes, music, pageantry, and performance.

your
place in TIME
20th Century America
What a Century It Was!
Technology...
changed our lives.
made our generations unique.
gave us shared memories.
Come on in and find
Your Place in Time!
Sponsored by
Popular Mechanics
The Road to Happiness

In Henry Ford Museum, a new generation of experiences focused on American ideas and innovations and featured motion and simulation, theatrical physical environments, and participatory opportunities. Some exhibitions, like *Your Place in Time: 20th Century America*, were thematic, while others, like *Heroes of the Sky: Adventures in Early Flight, 1903–1939*, reshaped a display of objects into an interpretive framework that told a story.

A new museum gallery for temporary exhibitions, which opened in 2003, allowed the museum to bring in traveling exhibitions as well as create its own temporary exhibits using its collections. The gallery hosted traveling "blockbusters" with mass appeal during the summer travel season while museum staff created more focused shows using The Henry Ford's collections during the "shoulder seasons." In spring 2005, for example, the gallery hosted *Vintage Couture*, featuring the fashions of Elizabeth Parke Firestone from its collections. *Baseball as America*, produced by the National Baseball Hall of Fame and Museum, entertained the summer visitors of 2006.

A grant from the Americana Foundation allowed staff to experiment with different forms of interpretation in an upgraded furniture gallery. *Fully Furnished* included a 1950s living room setting where visitors could actually pick up telephones to hear different family members discuss their opinion of the room's furnishings.

(Opposite) Through the immersive environments and multisensory experiences of *Your Place in Time: 20th Century America* (1999), visitors looked at how five generations coming of age during the twentieth century were shaped by the technologies of their formative years. As part of their research, the exhibit team interviewed members of each of the five generations.

(Next two pages) The completed *Dymaxion House—A New Way of Living* (2001) first took visitors through a factory setting like the one in which Fuller's prototype house was originally on view, then through a guided tour of the house itself.

EXIT
Spacious

8 D
Open House
Today!

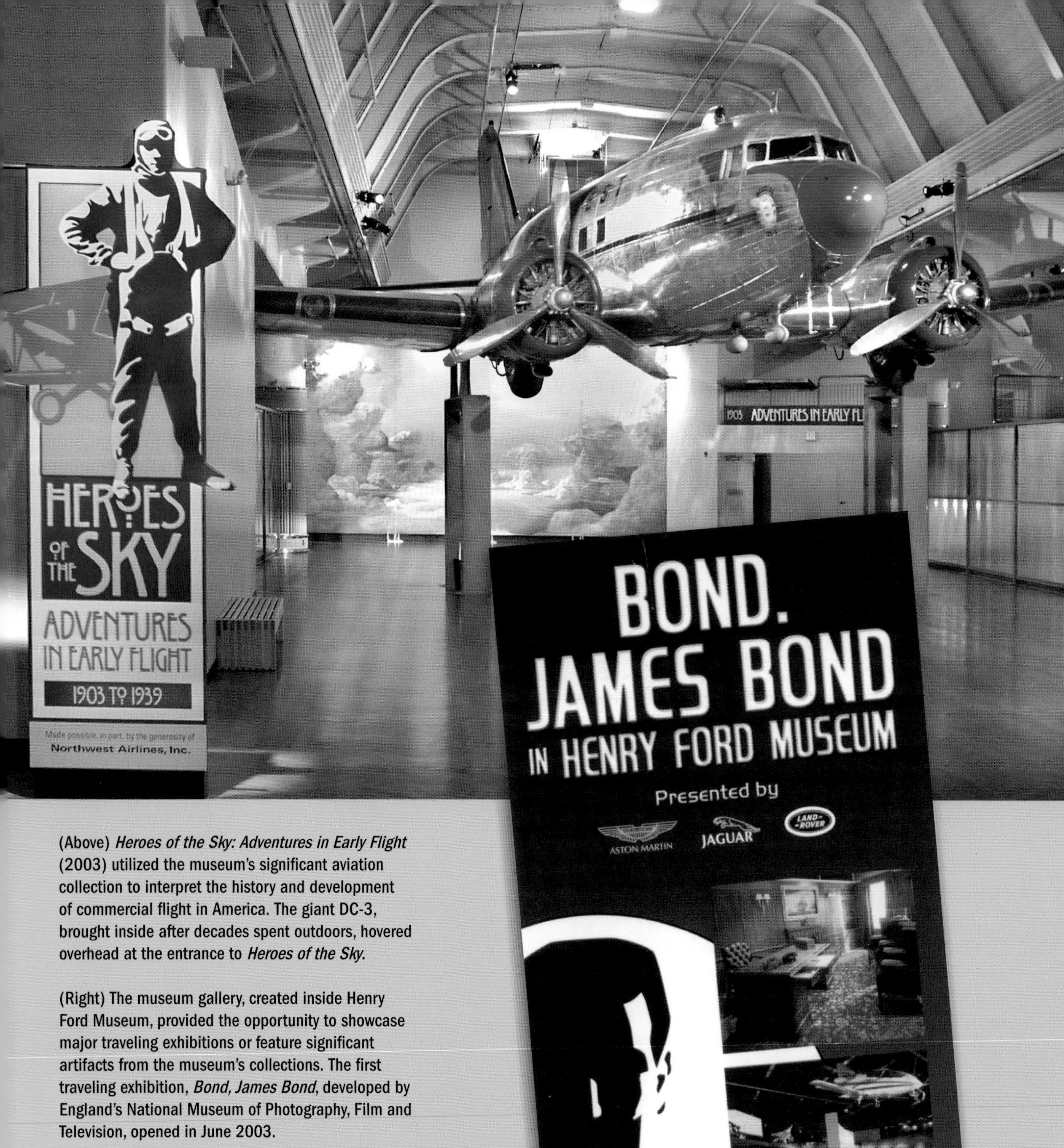

(Above) *Heroes of the Sky: Adventures in Early Flight* (2003) utilized the museum's significant aviation collection to interpret the history and development of commercial flight in America. The giant DC-3, brought inside after decades spent outdoors, hovered overhead at the entrance to *Heroes of the Sky*.

(Right) The museum gallery, created inside Henry Ford Museum, provided the opportunity to showcase major traveling exhibitions or feature significant artifacts from the museum's collections. The first traveling exhibition, *Bond, James Bond*, developed by England's National Museum of Photography, Film and Television, opened in June 2003.

(Above) *With Liberty and Justice for All*, which opened on Martin Luther King Day in 2006, utilized some of the most treasured national artifacts in the museum's collection to explore the struggles that arose in the quest for freedom in America. The exhibition included sections devoted to Independence, Freedom and Union, Votes for Women, and the Civil Rights Movement. Pictured here is a decorated Model T in the Votes for Women section of the *With Liberty and Justice for All* exhibition.

(Above) A temporary exhibit, *Quilting Genius 2,* featured the newly acquired improvisational quilts of Susana Allen Hunter, a quilter from rural Alabama.

(Below) A temporary exhibit, *Rock Stars' Cars & Guitars 2*, enlivened the summer of 2009. The exhibit featured a wall of guitars belonging to famous rock musicians.

the Henry Ford IMAX Theatre

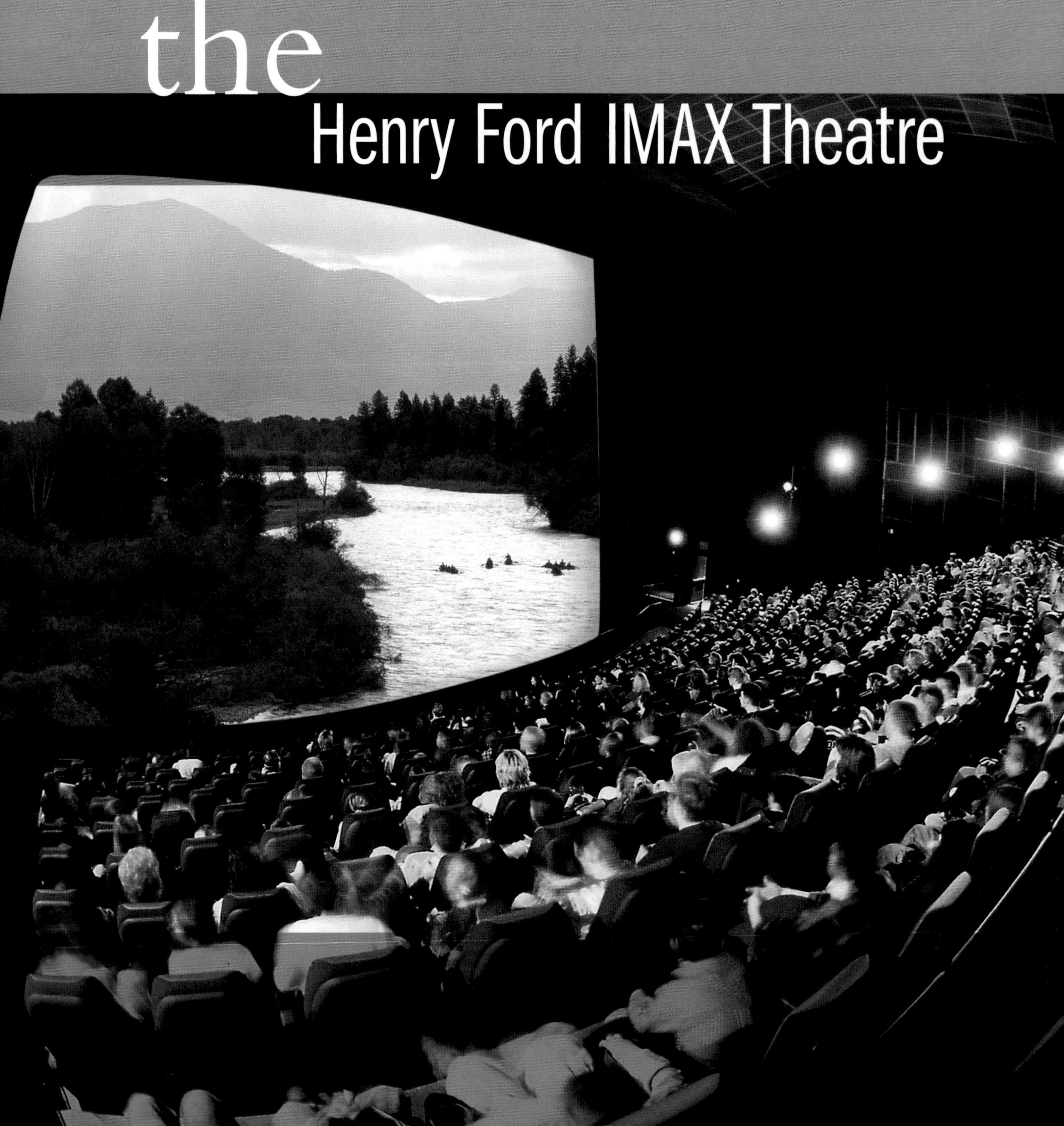

The IMAX Theatre "is a declaration to the world that a new Henry Ford Museum is emerging."

– *Detroit Free Press*, November 15, 1999

For several years, the museum had contemplated the addition of an IMAX Theatre as a way to attract new audiences—both local and from out of town—that are drawn to the large format film experience as well to extend the stay of existing visitors.

With the addition of the IMAX Theatre, the museum added a new lobby and entrance area to complement the physical improvements to the museum building. The 442-seat theatre was the first theatre in Michigan capable of showing both regular and 3-D films and the largest in the state. It opened to the public in November 1999. The program offerings ranged from educational films in regular and 3-D format to Hollywood features reformatted for the IMAX technology.

(Above) The visitor reception area at night beckoned customers to the IMAX Theatre.

(Left) The showing of *Fantasia 2000*, in the theatre's first year of operation, broke worldwide records for advance ticket sales.

(Opposite) Breathtaking images came alive on the six story-high IMAX screen, enhanced by powerful wrap-around digital sound.

benson

"The Benson Ford Research Center represents years of pursuing a goal and seeking a better way to preserve and provide access to our collections."

– Judith E. Endelman, Director, Benson Ford Research Center, *Living History*, Winter 2002

In March 2002, the museum dedicated the 66,000-square-foot Benson Ford Research Center, the cornerstone of the museum's historical content and research collections.

Benson Ford, whose children, Lynn Alandt and Benson Ford Jr., were the primary donors, was the second son of Edsel and Eleanor Ford, and a museum trustee for thirty-six years. He also served as chairman of the museum's board for four years after Henry Ford's death in 1947.

Two independent departments had merged in the late 1970s to create the Archives and Library, which ultimately became the Benson Ford Research Center. The archives began in 1964 when Ford Motor Company donated its corporate archives to form the nucleus for one of the most significant business archives and automotive history collections in the country. The addition of the Henry Austin Clark automotive history and other major acquisitions enhanced the significance of the automotive history holdings.

The museum's library (which became the Tannahill Research Library in 1970, in honor of a trustee, Robert H. Tannahill) began with collections of Ford's beloved McGuffey Readers, product literature, books, magazines, prints, posters, and other printed material, as well as manuscript collections, many associated with the buildings collected for Greenfield Village. The collections of product literature, posters, prints, and ephemera are among the finest in the country.

Students, scholars, educators, journalists, hobbyists, and other "free-choice" learners are all accommodated in the research center's reading room. The research center also sponsors lectures, book signings, conferences, internships, and research grants.

(Opposite) The Benson Ford Research Center's prominent location on the Josephine Ford Plaza.

(Right) A painting of the Ford Rotunda and a weather vane hang in the research center's storage area.

(Below) Pictured here are shoes from the couture collection of Elizabeth Parke Firestone.

The rich and extensive holdings of the Ford Motor Company are the largest of the Benson Ford Research Center's holdings. In the mid-1990s, the museum and the company began looking at ways to jointly preserve the record of Ford's history. These discussions culminated in December 2001, when the museum and Ford Motor Company announced the creation of the Ford Historical Resources Collaborative, to provide collaborative oversight of Ford's historic resources and confirm the Benson Ford Research Center as the primary source for understanding the history of Ford Motor Company. This innovative partnership was unique among corporate archives.

(Above and left) The research center storage includes storage areas for archival holdings, the library collection, and artifacts, the equivalent of five miles of shelving.

greenfield village Reborn

"My grandfather would have approved of this."

– William Clay Ford commenting on the Greenfield Village restoration project, 2002

More than seventy years of daily operation in Greenfield Village had taken its toll.

The infrastructure was crumbling and desperately in need of repair and reconstruction. In what was originally conceived as a multiyear initiative, the infrastructure improvement project was completed in nine short months.

Through a partnership with the Association of Underground Contractors (AUC)—Michigan's Heavy Construction Association—key contractor members contributed their time and expertise, significantly reducing the initial project estimate for the restoration through value engineering, direct contributions, and other cost-saving recommendations. To benefit from AUC's contribution, the project had to be done all at once and during the heavy construction industry's slow season—winter. Greenfield Village closed to the public in September 2002 and reopened in June 2003. During that period, which coincided with one of the coldest winters on record, thirty-five miles of underground systems were replaced, ten buildings were relocated, and new roads and sidewalks were laid.

New road is paved near Cotswold Cottage, April 2003.

That was only the beginning. The "reborn" village also featured a redesigned entry plaza, seven newly organized thematic districts, a millpond, and a new catering pavilion. In 2004, the Greenfield Village restoration won an award for Outstanding Achievement in the Extreme Makeover category from the Themed Entertainment Association.

(Opposite) Workmen removed entire roadways—and every water main, sewer pipe, electric line, and natural gas line beneath them. In some parts of the village, deep holes had to be dug where underground junctions of sewer and storm drains would meet. In this scene, workmen laid conduit near Richart Wagon Shop and the Soybean Laboratory in January 2003.

(Above) In the revamped Henry Ford's Model T district, guests could trace the life, work, and vision of Henry Ford, then take a test ride in a Model T.

For the grand reopening of Greenfield Village, Governor Jennifer Granholm and museum president Steven K. Hamp officially "cut" the ribbon to Greenfield Village by driving a Model T through it.

(Above) The new Village Pavilion, modeled after a western fort that provided shelter for travelers on the Overland Trail, offered a picturesque spot for private catered functions and a spacious location for public programs.

(Left) Hundreds of new lampposts in Greenfield Village, with distinctive designs to fit the look and feel of each district, made it easy to hold evening events any time of the year. Their light levels could be adjusted to set different moods. These lampposts surround the pond in Liberty Craftworks.

(Below) As a thank you for their generous contributions to the project, the contractors who worked on the Greenfield Village restoration and their families enjoyed a special opening night party in June 2003.

FACT:
The Greenfield Village restoration project included planting 25,000 trees, adding 350 new lampposts, replacing thirty-five miles of underground systems, building eleven miles of roads and sidewalks, constructing three new buildings, and relocating ten historic buildings.

ford Rouge Factory Tour

The Ford Rouge Factory Tour is "truly a glimpse at our industrial, labor-intensive past and a telescope into the knowledge and information age of our future."

– Tom Watkins, *Detroit News*, May 1, 2004

Through the early 1980s, the Detroit-based automotive companies offered public factory tours.

Concerns over liability and industrial spying eventually closed the tours, and the public's desire to watch a moving vehicle assembly line went unfulfilled.

In the late 1990s, when Ford Motor Company began planning a new F-150 truck assembly plant at its historic Rouge River Plant, the company in dialogue with The Henry Ford decided to incorporate a factory tour into the design. Henry Ford began construction of the massive Rouge complex in 1917. When it was completed in 1928, the Rouge was the largest industrial facility in the world. It became a National Historic Landmark District in 1978. The company was proud of the historic importance of the site and wanted visitors to learn the history as part of their factory tour. The company asked The Henry Ford to conceptualize and develop the tour experience, films, and exhibits for the new truck plant. Together, Ford Motor Company and The Henry Ford created an experience and tour through the final assembly portion of the Dearborn Truck plant complete with an elevated public walkway and visitor center.

A ride nearly eighty feet up in an elevator to the Observation Deck offers a panoramic view of the entire Rouge site, and features a bird's-eye view of the assembly plant's innovative "living roof" and demonstrations of other environmentally sensitive elements of the assembly plant design. The environmental innovations have encouraged wildlife to return. Some of the birds that call the living roof, wetland, and orchard habitats home include red-winged blackbirds, killdeer, and several types of ducks.

(Opposite) The experience began with a bus tour from the museum to the Ford Rouge complex.

The tour came to an end in the Legacy Gallery, where visitors could see five vehicles made at the Rouge that changed Ford Motor Company and automobile history: the Model A, the V-8, the 1949 Coupe, the Thunderbird, and the Mustang.

The Ford Rouge Factory Tour, managed by The Henry Ford, opened to the public in May 2004 and was an immediate success. Its Rouge Visitor Center won an Award for Outstanding Achievement from the Themed Entertainment Association. It also won a 2004 American Institute of Architects Award of Honor for Sustainable Design. The U.S. Green Building Council awarded the Rouge Complex a LEED (Leadership in Energy and Environmental Design) Award, validation of its sustainable, environmentally responsible design.

Today, the Ford Rouge Factory Tour allows visitors to explore American auto manufacturing history and innovation with two special films, and a tour through the Dearborn Truck Plant where they can watch the final assembly of the Ford F-150. An observation deck gives visitors a view of the entire Rouge complex as well as the world's largest living roof that covers the plant.

T3E32R
1FTR X12 W0 4F A00643
9610 SUP XLT
4x2 A G 3 ABP
A A 2 G
2 A B Y 1
B 1 S Y
B

"I met Bill Ford on January 14, 1999, and we went up to his office–which was on the top floor [of Ford World Headquarters], and looked out at the Rouge in the distance. And he asked me, 'Do you think you can apply your ideas to that place?' And I remember thinking, 'If we can't, you know, we're all dead,' because this has to become a living thing, instead of a dead and dirty thing."

– Bill McDonough, architect of the Dearborn Truck Plant, "Collecting Innovation Today" Interview, September 2008

(Opposite) Although videos along the walkway complemented the work of the assembly line, visitors preferred to come when they could watch the actual work going on.

The Art of Manufacturing Theater allowed visitors to experience modern-day manufacturing through a multisensory theater experience.

focusing on the Future

"I don't think I've ever been so 'jazzed' over a ragtime event as I was this weekend. Plain and simple, it was true Americana."

– Performer comment, quoted in Annual Report, 2007

In late 2005, Steve Hamp resigned as president of The Henry Ford to take a temporary assignment as chief of staff for William Clay Ford Jr., then the chairman and CEO of Ford Motor Company.

The country's economy had started to take a downward turn and the automotive companies—specifically, Ford, General Motors, and Chrysler, all headquartered in the Detroit region—began to face major challenges.

With Hamp's resignation, The Henry Ford's board of trustees appointed Patricia Mooradian as the institution's next president. As COO, she had led the development of a new ten-year strategic plan for the institution focusing on increased attendance, new educational products, visitor experiences, and new revenue. She re-branded and re-positioned the institution as a national destination with a new campus name—The Henry Ford—and integrated the master plans and processes for the $65 million restoration of Greenfield Village and the transformation of Henry Ford Museum. Mooradian also led the creative team responsible for the development of the Ford Rouge Factory Tour.

The Henry Ford's president Patricia Mooradian and a costumed presenter, Meeta Martin, examined some of the heritage plants grown in the Susquehanna House garden in Greenfield Village. Authenticity in program presentation continues to be a high priority.

(Opposite) The Ragtime Street Fair included lots of music, parades, costumed presenters, and audience participation.

As president, she refined and focused the organization's strategic plan around three significant core strategies—to transform Henry Ford Museum into a new, re-imagined experience; create a new paradigm for increased earned revenue; and expand and improve the institution's educational products.

"You are a leader in the field in providing the best possible museum services and experiences, reminding both your peers and the public exactly how much museums really matter in communities."

-Kim Igoe, interim president and CEO, American Association of Museums commenting on The Henry Ford's successful accreditation review, December 2006

The reconstruction and renewal of Greenfield Village in 2002–2003 had created a platform that supported rich, immersive visitor experiences. Existing programs, such as Holiday Nights, the Salute to America concerts with the Detroit Symphony Orchestra, and others, benefited from the multitude of improvements. A new special weekend, the Ragtime Street Fair, introduced in July 2007, took advantage of the improved sound system, street lighting, and newly paved sidewalks and roads to provide a weekend of live and recorded music, dancing, and a rousing New Orleans–style jazz parade to end the evening.

Now, the same care and attention needed to be devoted to Henry Ford Museum so that it could fulfill its promise to visitors to "discover how American ingenuity has transformed the way we live." The museum master plan, approved in 2007, called for an improved and updated *Automobile in American Life* exhibition, and new exhibits on American auto racing, innovation, and design. It also proposed improvements to the museum's infrastructure, visitor amenities, and way-finding.

One of the primary goals of the new strategic plan was to increase the percentage of annual earned income by exploring new sources of revenue. Senior staff fostered an entrepreneurial spirit, and many revenue initiatives sprang up across the institution.

Expansion and improvement of The Henry Ford's educational products and programs includes an intensified focus on web delivery of curriculum materials that use the museum's collections to create products that directly meet the state's educational requirements.

(Above) In the summer of 2008, actor and director Clint Eastwood filmed his feature-length film *Gran Torino* in the Detroit region. He and his wife, actress Dina Eastwood, enjoyed a visit to Greenfield Village one summer evening with president Patricia Mooradian, photographed here next to Clint Eastwood. During his visit, Eastwood commented that The Henry Ford, "far exceeded my expectations."

(Right) In October 2009, journalist and First Lady of California Maria Shriver broadcast an *NBC Nightly News* special report on "A Woman's Nation" from the floor of Henry Ford Museum. She is pictured here with Patricia Mooradian.

"The Henry Ford Museum [is] my bible. That's the greatest museum in the world for a car person."

– Jay Leno, *Detroit News*, March 11, 2009

(Above) During a visit to Detroit in April 2009, comedian Jay Leno toured The Henry Ford's car collection. Here he checks out the inner workings of a 1924 Doble steam car.

(Below) Executive chef Nick Seccia and Cathy Cwiek, manager of Historic Foodways and Domestic Life, examine freshly cut herbs in the Daggett Farmhouse garden. Seccia and the food service staff have developed relationships with dozens of local farmers and food suppliers. They also use herbs grown in village gardens for meals served at A Taste of History and Eagle Tavern restaurants.

"We're not reinventing cooking. But we're determined to offer new options for visitors—healthier, historic, and unique to what we do here at The Henry Ford."

– Nick Seccia, Executive Chef, *Time Traveler*, 2009-2010

(Above) The redesigned museum plaza incorporates the original cornerstone, signed by Thomas Edison in 1928, and provides entries into the major exhibits that surround it. A film of the dedication plays on a screen in front of the cornerstone.

(Right) A recent addition to the museum's furniture gallery focuses on the work of Ray and Charles Eames. It includes this beat-up-looking prototype for their iconic and ubiquitous fiberglass shell-shaped chairs that went into production in 1950.

(Far left) In 2006, The Henry Ford published its first Holiday Catalog, featuring crafts made in Greenfield Village and other custom and special products.

(Left) In 2008, the centennial of the Model T, The Henry Ford collaborated with two publishers to produce two histories of the Model T, one of them written by the museum's transportation curator, Bob Casey. It was named a Michigan Notable Book for 2008.

(Below) For years, the Village glassblowers produced authentic reproductions of nineteenth-century glassware. More recently, they have expanded their repertoire to include products inspired by a wide range of historic and classic contemporary glassware designs.

on Innovation

"At The Henry Ford, we don't just collect objects that tell the story of great innovations past; we seek to identify enduring principles to help new generations imagine and build the future."

–Patricia Mooradian, OnInnovation press release, May 28, 2009

Since its founding in 1929, The Henry Ford has amassed an unparalleled collection of artifacts representing American innovation and stories from some of the greatest innovators that ever lived, across multiple fields and disciplines, ranging from agriculture and industry to domestic life, transportation, and power generation.

OnInnovation.com, which launched in February 2010, connects the public with the stories of today's innovators.

(Opposite) Patricia Mooradian with Intel Corporation co-founder and chairman emeritus Gordon Moore at his interview for the "Collecting Innovation Today" oral history project. The pioneer work of Moore and others created "Silicon Valley"—as the region south of San Francisco became known—as a center of innovation in computer technology.

With a mission to inspire future generations to create a better tomorrow, The Henry Ford is a significant resource for understanding the history of American innovation. In 2007, as the global economy began to decline and some questioned America's ability to retain its innovative edge, The Henry Ford began to evaluate its role in re-defining and advancing the country's culture of innovation.

Not content to merely collect the artifacts and stories of historical innovators, The Henry Ford adopted an Innovation Platform as an essential component of its brand identity and value. The goals of this initiative were to promote the emergence of a new talent base of innovative thinkers by giving them historical context with which to pursue their ideas, to encourage creative problem-solving, and to inspire future generations with the stories of innovative achievers, both historical and contemporary, who devised radically new ways of doing things to produce a better result.

(Right) Charles Elachi during his interview for "Collecting Innovation Today" at NASA's Jet Propulsion Laboratory Museum. Elachi, vice president of the California Institute of Technology and director of the Jet Propulsion Laboratory, believes that new frontiers, in space and on Earth, cannot be conquered without taking risks and sometimes experiencing failure.

(Below) Mitchell Baker, chairperson, Mozilla Foundation, pictured here with Judith Endelman, was interviewed at Mozilla's headquarters for "Collecting Innovation Today." A fierce champion of the open-source movement, Baker leads a talented, largely volunteer workforce who share her commitment to keeping the Internet open and free.

"When I go and visit a museum like the Ford Museum, I'm absolutely fascinated with 'how did they start those first machines?' . . . I think preserving the evolution of our knowledge is something fundamental . . . to learning something about the future."

- Charles Elachi, director, Jet Propulsion Laboratory, "Collecting Innovation Today" Interview, February 2009

One component of the Innovation Platform was an oral history project to collect and then share the stories of contemporary innovators through a new website developed by the institution. This site, OnInnovation.com, launched in February 2010 and serves as a content- and resource-rich hub for anyone seeking to bring the power of perspective to their own innovation activities—whether in business, in the classroom, or in everyday life.

The institution's first interview was with racing legend Lyn St. James and was recorded during The Henry Ford's all-staff conference in 2008. By late 2009, the team had recorded thirty oral histories of some of the most creative thinkers and risk-takers in the computer industry, space exploration, industrial design, sustainable architecture, engineering, and auto racing.

As The Henry Ford looks to the future, its mission remains unchanged. The Henry Ford encourages people to learn from history and use those lessons to imagine and create a better world. Henry Ford's vision was to create an institution that celebrates common-day heroes, dreamers, and risk-takers—the people who have dared to change the world. Today, Ford's vision is alive and well as The Henry Ford continues to inspire a new generation of thinkers and doers to embrace the spirit of American innovation.

"The Henry Ford will be a nationally recognized destination and force for fueling the spirit of American innovation and inspiring a 'can-do' culture."

- The Henry Ford's vision statement 2010

(Below) At the March 2009 board of trustees meeting, William Clay Ford Jr. stepped down as chairman, a position he held for thirteen years. S. Evan Weiner became the first person from outside the Ford family to serve as chairman of the board. Sheila Ford Hamp, a twenty-eight-year trustee and former chairman, was elected vice-chairman. Christopher Hamp, the son of Sheila and Steve Hamp, became the first member of his generation to join the board of trustees. Pictured here, left to right: Christopher Hamp, Sheila Ford Hamp, S. Evan Weiner, and Patricia Mooradian.

bibliographic Essay

The sources for this book can all be found in the Benson Ford Research Center at The Henry Ford. The research center's holdings include Henry and Clara Ford's papers, the records of Ford Motor Company through the mid-1950s, and the archives of The Henry Ford, which include the records of the Edison Institute Schools and the Henry Ford Academy.

An important source of information for the early years are the "Reminiscences," a collection of nearly four hundred interviews with friends and associates of Henry Ford, conducted and transcribed in the early 1950s under the supervision of Owen W. Bombard. Interviews with Hayward Ablewhite, Fred Black, Edward Cutler, Ernest Liebold, Israel Sack, and others are all important sources of information on the origins and early development of the museum.

The museum's archives contain clippings, articles about the museum, museum publications, such as the *Greenfield Villager*, the *Herald*, annual reports, program brochures, internal memos, photographs, and films. The Henry Ford's registrarial records include information about donations and acquisitions to the collections.

The following list includes books and articles about The Henry Ford, as well as publications with significant sections devoted to The Henry Ford's history:

American Ingenuity: Henry Ford Museum and Greenfield Village. New York: H. N. Abrams, 1985.

An American Invention: The Story of Henry Ford Museum & Greenfield Village. Dearborn, MI: The Museum and Village, 1999.

Bernays, Edward L. *Biography of an Idea*. New York: Simon and Schuster, 1965.

Bryan, Ford R. *Clara: Mrs. Henry Ford*. Dearborn, MI: Ford Books, 2001.

———. *Henry's Attic: Some Fascinating Gifts to Henry Ford and His Museum*. Dearborn, MI: Ford Books, 1995.

———. *Henry's Lieutenants*. Detroit: Wayne State University Press, 1993.

Bryk, Nancy Villa. "Reports of our Death Have Been Greatly Exaggerated: Reconsidering the Curator." *Museum News*, March/April 2001, 38–41, 67–71.

Conn, Steven. *Museums and American Intellectual Life, 1876–1926*. Chicago: University of Chicago Press, 1998.

Greenfield Village and the Henry Ford Museum. New York: Crown Publishers, 1972, 1978.

A Home for Our Heritage: The Building and Growth of Greenfield Village and Henry Ford Museum, 1929–1979. Dearborn, MI: Henry Ford Museum Press, 1979.

An Illustrated History: Henry Ford Museum & Greenfield Village. Dearborn, MI: The Museum and Village, 1990, 1993 (2d edition).

"Inspiring Change: Post-Heroic Management: An Interview with Harold Skramstad and Steve Hamp at the Henry Ford Museum." *Museum News*, Jan./Feb. 1995, 32–56.

Kammen, Michael G. *Mystic Chords of Memory: The Transformation of Tradition in American Culture*. New York: Knopf, 1991.

Lankton, Larry. "Something Old, Something New: The Reexhibition of the Henry Ford Museum's Hall of Technology." *Technology and Culture* 21 (1980): 594–613.

Morton, H. F. *Strange Commissions for Henry Ford*. York, UK: Herald Printing Works, 1934.

Rentzhog, Sten. *Open Air Museums: The History and Future of a Visionary Idea*. Kristianstad, Sweden: Jamtli Förlag and Carlsson Bokförlag, 2007.

Skramstad, Harold. "An Agenda for American Museums in the Twenty-first Century." *Daedalus* 128 (1999): 109–128.

Staudenmaier, John. "Clean Exhibits, Messy Exhibits: Henry Ford's Technological Aesthetic." In *Industrial Society and Its Museums, 1890–1990: Social Aspirations and Cultural Politics,* edited by B. Schroeder-Gudehus. Langhorne, PA: Harwood Academic Publishers, 1993.

———. "The Giant Awakens: Revising Henry Ford's History Book." *Technology and Culture* 29 (1988): 118–124.

Watts, Steven. *The People's Tycoon: Henry Ford and the American Century*. New York: Knopf, 2005.

photo Credits

All photographs are by The Henry Ford staff photographers except for those on the following pages:

p. 2 (background and lower right) Michelle Andonian.

p. 3 (lower right) Andonian.

pp. 4–5 Andonian.

p. 9 Andonian.

p. 84 Philippe Halsman.

p. 104 (top) Halsman.

p. 105 (upper right) Halsman.

p. 116 Andonian.

p. 131 (lower right) Andonian.

p. 157 (top) Andonian.

p. 159 (top) Andonian.

p. 162 (top) Andonian.

p. 166 (top) White House photographer.

p. 168 Andonian.

p. 172 (bottom) White House photographer.

p. 175 Andonian.

p. 177 (top left and bottom) Andonian.

p. 183 (top right) Andonian, (bottom) Gary Malerba.

pp. 187–188 Andonian.

p. 189 (top) Andonian.

pp. 195–197 Andonian.

p. 201 Andonian.

p. 203 (bottom) Andonian.

p. 205 (bottom) Andonian.

pp. 206–209 Andonian.

index

about the Authors

Author and editor Judith E. Endelman is director of the Benson Ford Research Center at The Henry Ford. Her publications include *An American Experience: Adeline Moses Loeb (1876–1953) and Her Early American Jewish Ancestors* (co-author); *The Model T Reconsidered: Proceedings from the World of the Model T Conference* (editor); *Americans on Vacation* (co-author); *Religion in Indiana: A Guide to Historical Resources* (co-author); and *The Jewish Community of Indianapolis, 1849 to the Present.*

Author Jeanine Head Miller is curator of domestic life at The Henry Ford. She was a co-author of *An American Invention: The Story of Henry Ford Museum & Greenfield Village* and *Henry Ford: A Pictorial Biography* (as Jeanine M. Head).

Author Donna R. Braden is a curator and experience developer at The Henry Ford. Her publications include *Behind the Magic: 50 Years of Disneyland* (co-author), *Americans on Vacation* (co-author), *Leisure and Entertainment in America, Eagle Tavern Cookbook*, and *Streamlining America* (co-author).

Author Nancy E. Villa Bryk is director of education and public programs at the Ann Arbor Hands-On Museum. She was a co-author of *An American Invention: The Story of Henry Ford Museum & Greenfield Village.* Bryk previously served as curator of domestic life at The Henry Ford.

Editor Wendy Metros is director of media and film relations at The Henry Ford. She serves as editor for most of The Henry Ford's promotional publications, including *The Henry Ford*, an illustrated souvenir book, published in 2008.

telling America's Story
A History of The Henry Ford

Made in
America
Your Place in Time
Museum Gallery
Dymaxion House